More ONTARIO GHOST STORIES

Maria Da Silva & Andrew Hind

GHOST HOUSE

Ghost Hous

© 2012 by Ghost House Books
First printed in 2012   10 9 8 7 6 5 4 3 2 1
Printed in Canada

The Distributor: Lone Pine Publishing
2311–96 Street
Edmonton, AB T6N 1G3
Canada

Websites: www.ghostbooks.net
www.lonepinepublishing.com

Library and Archives Canada Cataloguing in Publication

Da Silva, Maria
          More Ontario ghost stories / Maria Da Silva and
Andrew Hind.

ISBN 978-1-55105-887-0

          1. Ghosts--Ontario. 2. Haunted places--Ontario.
I. Hind, Andrew II. Title.

BF1472.C3D385 2012   133.109713   C2012-901378-1

Editorial Director: Nancy Foulds
Project Editor: Sheila Quinlan
Production Manager: Gene Longson
Layout and Production: Volker Bodegom, Janina Kürschner
Cover Design: Gerry Dotto

Photography: All photos are by Andrew Hind and Maria Da Silva except: p. 66, courtesy of Simcoe County Archives; and p. 174, courtesy of Parry Sound Public Library.

We acknowledge the financial support of the Government of Canada through the Canada Book Fund (CBF) for our publishing activities.

Canadian   Patrimoine
Heritage   canadien

PC: 1

Contents

Foreword

While many people associate ghost stories with tall tales, wildly imaginative yarns meant to frighten and chill, this book is not a work of fiction. It details true hauntings from across the province of Ontario. Each story has a strong tradition and historical foundation upon which to rest, and the eyewitness accounts that give the tales such weight are recorded as told to us with little artistic licence. It is our belief that while ghost stories should be dramatic, they should also be truthfully presented and, as much as possible, authenticated. As a result, we extensively researched every story presented within this book using archival material, newspapers and interviews with knowledgeable individuals. The most strenuous efforts have been made for accuracy, both in historical detail and in the retelling of our sources' paranormal encounters.

While this book has been laid to rest (so to speak), our explorations of the strange and the mysterious certainly have not come to an end. We are always looking for further stories to add to our files, and we welcome feedback and correspondence from readers regarding their own paranormal experiences. Maria can be reached at dasilvababy@hotmail.com, and Andrew can be reached at maelstrom@sympatico.ca.

Introduction

Throughout myth, legend, modern film and literature, and countless personal accounts, ghosts are the stuff of nightmares. They are the most enduring icons of fear; every culture has its own tradition of restless spirits lingering in defiance of death, tarrying upon the mortal world, reluctant to pass on to eternity. It's likely that our prehistoric ancestors huddled around blazing fires and, in hushed tones, shared terrifying stories of the dead rising from their graves to stalk them in the night. Ghost stories are timeless, the most universal form of storytelling. *More Ontario Ghost Stories* is our contribution to this cherished tradition.

Ontario is a vast province, so although we've been researching its ghosts and legends for almost a decade, in that time we've chronicled only a fraction of the literally thousands of stories we've come across. Undoubtedly, many more exist and are as yet unknown to us. This book, therefore, is not intended to be a comprehensive study of the subject. Instead, *More Ontario Ghost Stories* contains a selection of our favourite hauntings, richly detailed stories that blend eyewitness accounts, folklore and history.

To avoid repetition, we consciously decided to avoid stories that appeared in this book's two predecessors—*Ontario Ghost Stories* and *Ontario Ghost Stories: Volume II*, both by Barbara Smith—as well as those appearing in our own earlier paranormal volumes, *Cottage Country Ghosts* and *Ghosts of Niagara-on-the-Lake*. The result, we believe, is a fresh book that will chill audiences with original, never-before-published tales.

On occasion, we ourselves have felt the cold chill of fear while visiting the locations featured herein. These occasions are exhilarating because they validate our work. After all, it is one thing to write about ghosts and to sincerely believe in the supernatural, but until you actually experience something that is unexplainable and by definition paranormal, you never truly *know* the very things we invest so much time in researching actually do exist.

Yet it can be heart-wrenching as well, because a spirit trapped in our realm is unable to rejoin his or her loved ones in the afterlife. An earthbound soul defies the compact of our existence, which states that though we may lose family and friends, we can seek solace in the certainty that we'll be with them again one day upon death. As a result, every ghost is by nature tragic. In addition, there's the reality that most of the earthbound spirits that attach themselves to a person or to a place do so out of a sense of unhappiness. After all, a person who lived a fulfilled and contented existence usually rests peacefully. Those who cling to the land of the living even after death has claimed their body are usually compelled by fear, sadness, injustice, delusion or anger—powerful emotions that make ghosts worthy of our pity as much as our fascination.

Oftentimes, it's difficult to ascertain exactly why a spirit lingers after death. All we can do is guess. Our motivation for writing this book is far less elusive: we want to entertain readers. So crawl into bed, pull the blankets up high and enjoy. We just can't promise you'll have pleasant dreams tonight. And isn't that the point of a good ghost story?

Ghosts of Black Creek Pioneer Village

Thousands of people visit Toronto's Black Creek Pioneer Village every year, where they are entertained and educated by the costumed staff who recreate daily life as it would have been for our pioneer ancestors. But it's possible that re-enactors aren't the only ones reliving the past. As many as a dozen of the 30-odd heritage buildings on site are haunted by spirits of Ontario's past.

Black Creek Pioneer Village is situated on two farm lots, one once belonging to Johann Schmidt, who settled there in 1809, and the second once belonging to Daniel Stong, who arrived a few years later in 1816. The buildings that made up the Stong farmstead—the original log home, their second, more substantial frame house, a grain barn, a piggery and a smoke house—form the core of the village. As a result, there is a strong spiritual connection between the buildings and the land itself. This isn't just a recreated pioneer village; successive generations were born, lived, worked and ultimately died on the very land sightseers walk through. Their hardships, their successes and failures, their dreams and fears, all were tied to their farms, and it seems that something of their souls has been left behind.

The last descendants of the Stong family vacated the homestead in 1958 and sold their property to Metro Toronto Regional Conservation Authority to serve as part of Black Creek Pioneer Village. The park was opened to the public in 1960, and over the course of the next three decades a number of additional buildings of historical significance were added to the site. Apparently many of these structures brought spectral residents with them, long-dead souls bonded to wood and brick, creating a ghostly community at Black Creek.

When one stops to think about it, should it really come as any surprise that the park is haunted? After all, Black Creek Pioneer Village is a monument to all those settlers who came to a young Canada and carved our nation from the wilderness. Dramas full of hardships, endless toil, births and deaths, and always hope for a better future, took place within the walls of these historic buildings. Such strong emotional energies don't simply dissipate, and it's these energies that keep the ghosts tied to their former home or place of business. They're what make the park so vibrant.

In this chapter we share the shivers associated with three of Black Creek Pioneer Village's buildings: Burwick House, the Rose Blacksmith Shop and the Black Creek Cemetery.

Burwick House

Walking into the circa-1840 house, I instantly felt that there was something alluring about it, something I couldn't immediately put my finger on. As we entered through a front door ringed with evergreen boughs, it felt as though we were intruding upon someone's private holiday gathering. The place was decorated with the warmth of old Victorian charm. The table was set for dinner, the furniture was all in its place and the grandfather clock stood tall and proud as we passed it to walk up the staircase. Evergreen wreaths, a kissing ball and sprigs of berries and dried fruits added a sense of Christmas from years gone by. Wandering around this magnificent home was like being taken back in time. The Burwick home, I was certain, must surely have been inviting to anyone who was fortunate enough to attend the parties it hosted long ago.

The feeling of warmth and yuletide cheer began to seep away as I climbed the stairs. Something came over me as I approached the second floor. Step by step it grew stronger, more difficult to ignore. I felt the presence of a distraught woman, lingering like a dark shadow of pain of suffering. As I reached the top of the stairs, four rooms were visible: a pair of children's rooms, a sewing room and the one I seemed most drawn to, the master bedroom where husband and wife would have slept. A baby's crib stood to one side, and mourning clothes were laid upon the bed. Although it may have been merely an eerie coincidence, the bedroom seems to tell the tale of a family in grieving and has a distinctly melancholy atmosphere.

Was the woman I sensed in mourning for her baby? Was her spirit still looking for her child two centuries after fate cruelly snatched it from her arms? The presence was now uncomfortably strong and details came clear: the woman was between the ages of 20 and 30, too young to rightfully grieve the loss of a child. Her pain became overwhelming to me, and I felt the need to reach out to the grieving mother. To everyone else present—including my co-writer—there was no spectral woman in the bedroom, but I knew different.

The ghostly entity lingers in the room, tied to the cradle that will forever lay empty. In years past, when the sound of children's laughter came from the street outside, she would wander over to the window to get a glimpse of them. It must have been so painful to watch children happily playing when her own child had been tragically deprived of that joyful experience. I can only imagine the torment that this woman must have endured at those moments, but my heart ached for her. Any mother's would.

My experience at Burwick House profoundly shook me. I had to learn more about this place and the ghost trapped within. Somehow, I thought uncovering the story would ease the pain of this mourning ghost, and perhaps some of my own as well.

Burwick House was named for the village of Burwick (now Woodbridge, located just north of Toronto), which in turn was named for its founder, Rowland Burr. Burr was a carpenter by trade, but he made his fortune building mills and in land development. In 1837, he purchased 100 acres of unsettled forest along the Humber River and erected a sawmill, woollen mill and grist mill. These industries became the heart of a little village, named Burwick in his honour. As the village grew, Burr began subdividing his property into residential lots, occasionally also building homes for the new owners.

A ghostly woman remains trapped within Burwick House.

Robert Shannon was one of these newcomers. A wealthy wheelwright, in 1844 he had Burr build him a home that would reflect his privileged status within the small community. Burwick House was the result: a one-and-a-half-storey home that, thanks to an imposing face, looks much larger than it actually is. It certainly would have stood apart from the typical modest rural residences of the day.

Shannon resided in the home for a number of years, and it subsequently passed through various hands until it was finally purchased by the Bank of Montreal to serve as the Woodbridge branch. In 1958 the bank, recognizing the historic value of the building, donated Burwick House to Black Creek Pioneer Village in Toronto, making it one of the living history museum's original buildings. It's also one of the most attractive.

But there's more than just architecture and a sense of history that draws people to Burwick House. There is also the ghost. I wasn't alone in sensing her mournful presence; staff members have long reported mild poltergeist activity in the building, such as blankets pulled from the bed, a cradle that rocks on its own and unidentifiable knocking sounds coming from the walls. Some people have complained of random cold spots and a general unease in the home, an unsettling presence that hovers at the edge of their senses like a dark shadow. People climbing the stairs to the warm and elegant second floor bedrooms distinctly hear the sound of footsteps pacing across the upstairs floor, but upon reaching the landing they are startled to discover that they are alone. They may find a deep indentation in the centre of the bed in the master bedroom, as if someone (or something) had been sitting there just a few seconds earlier, heedless of the ropes that cordon off the room from the public.

Some spectral activity is less subtle. At night, the resident ghost is occasionally responsible for lighting up an upstairs window with a strange, glowing aura. Security guards who investigate never find anyone in the building, nor any explanation for the light. Some people sense the presence of the woman standing beside the crib. You may even catch a glimpse of her out of the corner of your eye, though the apparition usually vanishes if you look directly at her. One costumed staff member seated at the kitchen table was startled when she saw the dark shadow of a woman standing in the kitchen doorway. Moments later, the shadow merged with the darkness and was gone.

Almost all reports agree that the ghost is largely confined to the second floor bedrooms, and yet not all poltergeist activity occurs upstairs. Each of the eight rooms in the home is furnished with exquisite pieces, most of them in all likelihood brought over from the Old Country. But amongst the fine china, expensive furniture and Persian rugs, one item truly stands out—a beautiful, ornate grandfather clock. The clock may chime for no apparent reason or count off the hours inaccurately. Minor foibles perhaps, easily explained by aging machinery, except for one thing: the clock is no longer kept in operating condition.

So how would one explain a clock, which should not be working, that rings incessantly and seemingly without reason until a party of visitors vacates the upstairs? It's a question that, for one mother and her young daughter at least, couldn't be answered with reason. When they first began to climb the stairs, the pair felt nothing out of the ordinary. They were simply excited by their day's explorations and eager to see what awaited them upstairs in this beautiful old home. Soon after they reached the second floor, however, they began to feel cold and unwelcome. The young girl in particular was ill at ease. She felt a soft hand gingerly touch her face and momentarily cup her chin. And then the clock began to chime. It wasn't the peaceful ringing that is so endearing about grandfather clocks. Instead, it sounded ominous, almost agitated. Instinctively, the mother knew it was time to leave, and tightly gripping her child by the hand, she fled down the stairs. As soon as mother and child were safely downstairs, the clock stopped its chiming. It was as if the ghost was using the clock to voice her displeasure at the unwelcome intrusion into her domain.

Spurred by stories such as this, the Toronto and Ontario Ghosts and Hauntings Research Society, a non-profit organization founded in 1997, began to investigate the paranormal activity at Black Creek Pioneer Village. After conducting three informal visits, as well as various in-person and telephone interviews with staff members, the society members came away convinced that Burwick House is home to at least "mild poltergeist activity."

"We have first-hand reports of hauntings from descendants of the family that once lived in the house," said society member Sue Darroch, "but we've signed non-disclosure agreements and are unable to divulge information or names." At the same time, staff members at Black Creek Pioneer Village are often hesitant to discuss their experiences. "We have followed up on these reports to the best of our abilities, but we were informed during our last visit by one staff member that Black Creek Pioneer Village is attempting to move away from the stigma that old houses automatically equate to ghosts, and therefore many staff members may be reluctant to speak publicly about possible experiences."

We encountered the understandable reluctance ourselves. While everyone at Black Creek was hospitable and supportive of our work, and more than willing to provide historical information, it was somewhat harder to coax ghost experiences from them. When asked, workers were generally coy about the subject, at least on the record. One woman grinned knowingly and told us ghost stories weren't something they promoted. She then asked if we had seen the upstairs. Was that a hint? We took it as such.

One of those who was not only willing but also eager to share her story was "Marlee." She generously offered her unsettling story on the condition of anonymity. It was late into the evening by the time Marlee and a coworker began the short walk back to the administrative building after one of the park's rare nighttime events. The moon, which had been playing peek-a-boo with drifting clouds all night, poked through to cast the village in an eerie glow, causing deep shadows to stretch across the reproduction pioneer streets. Marlee found her eyes drawn to the second floor of Burwick House, where a pale white light shone in one of the windows. "It kind of flickered, like a candle sputtering in its own wax," she explains. "We were scared that an oil-lamp had been left on and went to investigate."

Marlee and her associate had no way of knowing that they were about to receive and an even greater scare. Pushing open the front door of Burwick House, Marlee immediately felt an ominous presence that caused her to pause in her steps. Regaining her composure, she began to climb the creaking stairs, but her knees grew weaker with each step taken. She reached the landing inexplicably exhausted by the short ascent. "There was no lamp burning, nor any other light source that would explain the glow we saw," Marlee explains. "But I saw a black figure, a shadow, walk across one of the bedrooms. It was only there for a moment, but it was definitely a woman."

A chill suddenly came over Marlee, and cold terror jolted through her body as her mind finally registered what she had seen. Her breath came in jagged gasps, and she reflexively gripped her friend's arm. "My coworker saw the panic in my face and quickly suggested we leave. She hadn't seen the ghost, but she did feel uneasy about something and was just as scared as I was."

Some encounters in Burwick House are a bit more ominous in nature, almost always when young children are present. It's as if the ghost is tormented by the sight of these kids, reminding her of all those precious experiences of parenthood that she never had in life, so many joys of watching children develop that were stolen away when her own child died. One woman who toured the home with her husband and children was overcome by "a horrible feeling of utter sadness and something very sinister" as she climbed the stairs. By the time she reached the top she was on the verge of a panic. "I felt very uneasy and wanted to leave immediately. I felt the hair on the back of my neck stand up," she said. Unnerved, the woman raced down the stairs and awaited her family outside.

An innocent young girl completely unaware of the paranormal aspect of Burwick House broke down in hysterics while exploring the home. Between sobs, she told her concerned parents that she felt someone touching the back of her shoulder, like the gentle guiding hand of a mother, while her back was against an open bedroom door. There had been no one there. On a separate occasion, another youthful girl felt the icy grip of a cold, invisible hand through her thick woollen mitten. It seems the mournful ghost, desperately missing her child, can't resist the urge to reach out from the other side to make physical connection with living visitors. The maternal instinct is undying, and the grief-stricken apparition remains tied to the room in which her baby slowly slipped from her loving arms into the cold embrace of death. Her presence is an eerie reminder of the tragedies that were commonplace in our nation's pioneer era.

The truth is, we don't know for certain who the spectral figure is. But for at least three witnesses, one thing is certain: a spectral young mother lingers within the home's comfortable confines, and her sadness remains raw to this day. In Burwick House, history truly does come alive, regardless of whether or not you believe in ghosts. To explore the elegant rooms of this home is to walk with those who came before us, to appreciate the lives they lived, and perhaps, if you're sensitive enough, to feel some of their loss. So if by chance, while touring Burwick House, you sense her presence or if your child feels the warm, soft caress of a gentle hand, don't be scared. It's just a heartbroken mother hoping to find her own child.

Rose Blacksmith Shop

An orange glow lit up the night sky, casting the village of Nobleton in an eerie light. Bedrooms across town were illuminated by the glow, rousing groggy villagers from their sleep. They stumbled out of bed and into the streets, their steps quickened by the sure knowledge that somewhere a building was aflame. None, however, were prepared for the horror that awaited them.

Intense flames were shooting up high through the roof of a stable. Above the crackling of the burning wood the aghast villagers could hear the panicked whinnies of horses trapped within. Several men raced forward to free the beasts, but the flames were so hot that the men couldn't even get close to the building and were forced to retreat across the street. They watched helplessly as the stable was consumed by fire, and even the burliest men found their eyes watering as they listened to the sound of the horses' agonized death throes. The smell of burnt flesh stung their noses, a gut-churning stench that few would ever forget.

When at last the fire played itself out, all that remained was charred timbers and mounds of ash. The fire had been so intense that the metal hinges on the doors had melted. The barn could be rebuilt, and in time would be, but the gentle, loving creatures inside could not so easily be replaced. So while it wasn't long before winds carried away the cooled cinders, the spirits of the dead horses remained bound to the charred timbers, trapped forever within the stables in which they perished. They're still there today, nearly two centuries later, even though the building, rebuilt as a blacksmith shop, has moved south to the grounds of Black Creek Pioneer Village.

During the day, the air within the Rose Blacksmith Shop is thick with smoke and the scent of burning coals; the almost oppressive heat of the forge's fire warms your face; the incessant ringing of hammer on anvil echoes as the smith shapes heated metal into a horseshoe. At night, when the oil lamps have been blown out in the village and visitors have long departed, an entirely different atmosphere pervades the building. An oppressive chill seeps out from its doorway, and some employees tell of unusual sounds emanating from the shadow-filled blacksmith shop. The noises vary: sometimes it's the clopping of horse hooves on wooden floorboards; sometimes it's the jingle of metal harnesses; and other times it's the soft whinnying, snorting and neighing of invisible horses. What's consistent is that the noises have no earthly cause, and the startled staff member unfortunate enough to hear them is left deeply disturbed.

In any 19th-century community, the blacksmith was one of the most important individuals. Almost every village had a blacksmith shop to serve local needs. In addition to forging horseshoes, the blacksmith was kept busy repairing farm equipment and wagon wheels, crafting a wide variety of tools and farm implements, and making household items such as pots and hinges. If the machinery at the local mill needed repair, the blacksmith was the one to call. In short, if the product was metal, a blacksmith was expected to be able to make and repair it. He was a craftsman essential to pioneer life.

Even today the blacksmith retains a nostalgic appeal. Among the more than a dozen authentically restored pioneer buildings on display at Black Creek Pioneer Village, the Rose Blacksmith Shop is arguably the most popular with visitors. If only they knew of the frightful, perhaps even vengeful ghosts that lurked within, or were aware of the origins of these restless spirits, perhaps visitors would not find it so alluring.

The Rose Blacksmith Shop originated in Nobleton, where it sat in the heart of the village and served as a village landmark for a century. It was built in 1855 as a stable for horses, using the charred framing timbers and foundations of the stable that had burned to the ground a few years earlier. The timber structure with board and batten finish was purchased by George Holden, who operated it as a blacksmith shop. Holden became a fixture in the community, highly regarded for his skill with a hammer and forge.

Holden's son, William Holden, apprenticed under his father and took over the business in 1906. He in turn passed his knowledge on to his grandson, Norman Rose, who became the last member of the family to operate the smithing business when he took over in 1938. By this date, even in rural Ontario blacksmiths were on the verge of obsolescence. Cars were succeeding horses on country roads, farming was becoming increasingly mechanized, and factory-made products had replaced those made by village craftsmen. Most blacksmith shops had disappeared, victims of changing times. Norman Rose resisted the tides of change for longer than most, but finally in 1958 even this stubborn gentleman realized the era of the blacksmith had drawn to an end and reluctantly hung up his hammer and let the fire in the forge die out.

Three years later, Norman Rose's tools and frame building were sold to Black Creek Pioneer Village and moved on site. There, the building was intended to preserve the legacy and trade of four generations of the

Holden family. Fittingly, Norman Rose was hired to work in the shop and remained as the village blacksmith until 1976, happily passing on his knowledge to eager tourists.

Many people suspect more than the forge and the craftsman that laboured upon it accompanied the blacksmith shop on its move to Black Creek Pioneer Village. It wasn't long before stories began to circulate that the sound of terrified horses neighing in panic and kicking desperately at stable walls could be heard echoing out of the shop late at night. According to long-standing lore, several horses perished in gruesome fashion in the fire that claimed the stables upon whose foundation the Rose Blacksmith Shop was built.

Several employees in the village know the spectral horses are more than just lore; they are in fact chillingly real. One long-standing employee, a respectable man who did not want to risk ridicule by sharing his name, swears he briefly heard the distinct sound of terrified horses coming from the shop. "It was as if they were trying to get free from some great danger," he asserted, firm in his conviction that it was not his imagination, nor the sound of flesh-and-blood horses. The employee was further adamant that he had never heard the legend of the spectral horses before his brief but unsettling experience. Although the sound was fleeting, the absolute panic he heard in the horses' cries burned into his memory. That experience, unnerving though it may have been, was actually tame compared to that of a night watchman. He was doing rounds late one evening when he heard the tortured, panicked wails of the long-dead horses.

The Rose Blacksmith Shop is tainted by the spirits of long-dead horses.

Visitors to the park have had their share of encounters as well. During a ghost tour of the village in 2007, tour guide and author Catherine Luscombe and the group she was leading that dark, chilly night had an unexpected experience of their own at the Rose Blacksmith Shop. Catherine gathered the dozen or so people around her in front of the building, holding her lantern up high to cast the small group in an eerie light. She watched as they subconsciously huddled together, seeking the courage of others in anticipation of a spine-tingling tale.

The doors to the blacksmith shop were wide open and there was a pair of candle lanterns burning inside, illuminating the shop in a feeble light. Although the forge, tables and tools hanging from the walls were visible in the gloom, deep shadows lurked menacingly in the depths of the building. It was dark and still, with no breeze. Catherine had just started to recount the story of the deadly stable fire when suddenly everyone turned to the blacksmith shop, eyes wide and hair standing on end.

"A distinct sound of jangling metal started clanging on the right-hand side of the shop, followed by a faint whinny sound," related Catherine. "Everyone with me on the tour heard it, and we all stopped talking and looked at each other in shocked silence. I was just as startled as everyone else. I had heard the tale before from employees, but I was actually hearing it for myself for the first time."

She continued. "There was no movement coming from inside the shop at all. Everything was still and there was nothing that could account for the sound. After about a minute of silence, very puzzled looks and some nervous laughter, I continued on with the ghost tale. I wasn't surprised at all when some people didn't follow me to the next building on the tour but stayed behind to see if they could hear the haunting horses in the blacksmith shop come to life once more."

Sometimes the ghost horses escape from the blacksmith shop and roam the village streets. The clopping of hooves and the jingle of harnesses have occasionally been heard outside the building, even on bright afternoons when ghosts and things that go bump in the night are far from people's minds. Because horses are not always on site, and only occasionally hitched to a wagon to offer visitors rides through the recreated village, there's usually no reasonable explanation for the sounds.

Marianna Lester had perhaps the most frightening encounter with the curse that taints the blacksmith shop.

She had been to Black Creek Pioneer Village many times over the years and had never witnessed anything unusual, let alone paranormal, in any of the restored buildings. There was always a distinctive spirit to each home and business, but Marianna knew that spirit came from stepping back in time to another era rather than from any souls that may have been lingering about. Her feelings about the place changed suddenly and dramatically when she took her grandfather to the museum a few years back.

"We experienced something really unusual at the blacksmith shop," she recounted via email. "My grandfather, who is from out of town, wanted to visit Black Creek, so I took him, my grandmother and my mother. We were standing in the shop. I was a distance off taking some photos while the three of them were by the entrance talking. All of a sudden, all three of them were startled to hear a horse neighing. They said that it sounded like the horse was right beside them, and of course there was no horse in the building."

Marianna's grandfather walked outside to look around, thinking maybe there was a horse hitched beside the building. He was surprised to find there wasn't. He walked around the entire building and even peered down the streets, looking for a horse that could have made the noise. He saw nothing. But sound carries, he reasoned, so perhaps there was a horse somewhere on the property. The three of them eventually shrugged off the experience, kept on with their conversation and enjoyed the remainder of a pleasant day in our pioneer past.

"Later, on our way out of the park, my grandfather asked if there were horses on site that day and they learned there weren't. Now he was really shocked, because all three were sure of what they had heard," wrote Marianna. "What I hadn't told them was that I had a startling experience as well. I was sure that, for a fleeting second, I had seen a large horse out of the corner of my eye while taking photos. It was right around the time my mother and grandparents thought they heard a horse whinny."

The horse Marianna saw was no normal horse, however, but rather a nightmarish monster with hide as black as pitch and eyes that burned red with the fires of hell. The image startled her, naturally, but of course there was nothing there so she dismissed it. She had been on a ghost tour of the park the year before and, unlike her mother and grandparents, knew the story of the undead horses reined for all eternity within the building. It was her imagination running wild, she reasoned.

Yet the experience lingered in the dark recesses of her mind and emerged, like a horror crawling up from a fresh-dug grave, while she slept. Her dreams were filled with that same terrifying horse. It was huge and black, with eyes full of anger and hate. It was enveloped in a cloud of reeking ash and smoke, and it almost roared when it reared up over her on its hind legs. Marianna ran as fast as she could, and the horse chased her through the village. There was no escape, and it felt as if the horse would overtake her at any moment. Finally, blessedly, she awoke covered in a cold sweat.

"It was just a nightmare, right? Except later on, when I developed my photos, there were orange orbs…almost like dancing flames…in some of the pictures I took in the blacksmith shop," Marianna said. "It sure felt real to all of us."

The horse she saw fleetingly by the blacksmith shop and more terrifyingly in her dreams was a dark, malicious reflection of the gentle creatures the real horses once were. Perhaps they have been twisted by the agonizing pain they experienced in their final moments, and by the discovery that their suffering now stretches on into eternity. They are filled with burning hate for the humans they once loyally served, angered by the fact that no one braved the smoke and flames to come to their rescue all those years ago.

Many people have had an experience of one kind or another with the smithy's spectral horses, but the most mysterious ghost haunting the Rose Blacksmith Shop is the spirit of a "man in black." In 2009, an employee was walking through the village with a pair of coworkers at the end of a long, humid summer day. She remembers that her long period dress seemed heavier and hotter than usual, and that she was exhausted and eager to get home. As they hustled toward the administration building on weary feet, she saw a man standing just inside the door of the blacksmith shop.

They were deep in conversation, and perhaps in her tired state she wasn't thinking as clearly as usual, so it took a few moments to dawn on her that she didn't recognize the individual. "Who was the guy in the blacksmith shop, the man dressed in black?" she asked. To her surprise, neither of her coworkers had seen him, and neither one knew of anyone new working at the village. When they inquired later, they discovered that there should not have been anyone in the blacksmith shop that day.

Who is the mysterious man in black? He isn't of this world, of that these women are certain. The employee who saw him leaning casually on the frame of the blacksmith shop's door is convinced she saw a ghost as dusk settled upon the village that day. Who that ghost might be is a puzzle to her, but it seems likely that he was one of three Holden men who laboured their lives away within the stifling confines of the building.

While other buildings at Black Creek Pioneer Village are more impressive and notable, few are more unforgettable than the humble Rose Blacksmith Shop. While watching a pioneer-era craftsman at work as he bends over a hot fire shaping metal with hammer, someone—something—unseen might just be watching you in return. You may even catch the sound of harnesses jingling or of hooves stomping on the wooden floor. And just as dusk falls on the historic buildings, the mournful cries of horses in abject terror and unimaginable pain may echo across the grounds, desperate for someone to come to their rescue.

Unfortunately, there is no saving them. They are beyond our ability to assist. Perhaps someday the flames fuelling their undead souls will die out and allow the horses to move over to the other side.

Black Creek Cemetery

Set at the rear of Black Creek Pioneer Village, shaded by trees and in the shadow of Fisherville United Church, is a modest cemetery. About a dozen humble plots, each marked with a simple headstone of weathered granite, sit among shrubbery and trees. There's a sense of sacred tranquility about the cemetery, a fittingly respectful atmosphere for the final resting place of pioneer settlers who once lived upon the land now occupied by the recreated 19th-century village.

And yet, it seems at least one individual interred within this graveyard has found no comfort in the afterlife. This spirit, an innocent boy taken far too early, lingers in the mortal world in defiance of death. Like any child, he spends most of his time playing and being mischievous, completely unaware that his youthful hijinks often leave his flesh-and-blood playmates—staff and tourists alike—startled and even frightened. He vanishes before he can be scolded, returning to his grave to nap and excitedly plot his next game.

Unlike most of the sites at Black Creek Pioneer Village, the cemetery is original to the location. It was established in 1859 to serve the farming hamlet of Kaiserville, located at the crossroads of Steeles Avenue and Finch Avenue. The cemetery was adjacent to the Townline Church, a modest log house of worship attended by Methodists. The church closed in 1884 but remained in use as a Sunday school for many years afterward. Eventually, the aging building fell into disrepair and was torn down.

When Black Creek Pioneer Village was founded, its organizers realized they needed to acquire a historic church to represent pioneer-era worship. They found an ideal candidate in the Fisherville United Church, built in 1856. Not only was this charming chapel of similar vintage to the lost Townline Church, but it also came from a village that was a direct neighbour to Kaiserville, located a few kilometres to the east at the intersection of Steeles Avenue and Dufferin Street. In 1960, Fisherville United Church was moved to its new home and erected on almost the exact spot where its predecessor had stood.

Although the church is a popular part of any visit to Black Creek Pioneer Village, the little cemetery is almost hidden from view and is often overlooked by visitors. This is perhaps appropriate; as the last resting place of many settlers of the old Kaiserville community, it shouldn't be treated as a tourist attraction. Unfortunately, this lack of visitation leaves the restless spirit of a young boy lonely and craving companionship. Consequently, he spends considerable effort drawing attention to himself: manifesting as ghostly orbs that bob and weave amidst the weary grey headstones of the cemetery, playing poltergeist pranks on unwary adults, playfully tugging on the clothes of unsuspecting people, and even appearing briefly during supernatural versions of hide-and-seek.

We know virtually nothing about this lad, except for the fact he lived in Kaiserville, died sometime during the 19th century and was buried within the cemetery. Sadly, his identity eludes us because his and many other grave markers have been destroyed or rendered illegible by the

elements over the years. We do know that he passed tragically young; the spirit is described as a child about
10 years old, wearing period clothes, with round cheeks
and a bright smile that wins the heart of almost everyone
who sees him. He's shy, however, and only rarely shows
himself. Most of the time, he makes his presence known
to the living in less obvious, but nonetheless mischievous, ways.

At times, for example, glowing lights are seen on the
cemetery grounds at night. Sometimes they are faint
pinpricks, like lightning bugs, while other times they take
the form of a bright orange glow, similar to a lantern's
flame, which illuminates the entire graveyard. The night
security employees at Black Creek Pioneer Village have,
on many occasions, reported seeing unexplained orbs
dancing and weaving among the graves, sometimes even
spilling out onto the dirt road that goes by the church.
These lights look as though they are chasing one another,
like children at play, and continue their game of tag for
minutes at a time.

One evening, one of these security guards brought
a German shepherd watch dog with him on his night
shift. He always felt better having his fearless dog at his
side, knowing that the dog's senses were far more acute
than his own and would sense danger well before he
would. In addition, a German shepherd is an intimidating
animal when riled; a person who might consider running
from or fighting against a security officer generally thinks
twice when confronted by 100 pounds of muscle and
bared teeth.

The ghost of a young boy haunts the Black Creek Cemetery.

Late into the night, with clouds fleeing like dark shadows across the moon, the guard snapped a leash on his dog and took him on patrol around the park. All was uneventful until they reached the back of the village in the vicinity of the church. As they approached the cemetery, the dog became agitated and started to growl and bark. The fur on his neck rose on end and his lips pulled back to reveal dagger-like teeth. The security guard looked from his dog to the darkened depths of the cemetery, concern draining the colour from his face. He swept the beam of his flashlight over headstones weary with age and into dense shrubbery, but he saw nothing out of the ordinary. And yet his dog continued to growl menacingly, clearly agitated, his heightened senses picking up something just beyond the range of the flashlight. The guard was frozen with anticipation—what was out there?

Suddenly the German shepherd hunched down and started to slink away from the area, tail between his legs and whining softly. The security guard thought grimly that it was time to go. "If whatever's lurking in the cemetery is spooking my dog, it's obviously best left alone," he said to himself. Together, dog and master backed away from the cemetery to complete their rounds of the rest of the village.

The man could never figure out what had frightened his dog. The rest of the evening went by uneventfully, and when he returned to the cemetery the next morning he found nothing unusual there. In fact, there was never anything reported—a vandal perhaps, or a robber—that would have alerted the dog. Something, however, had clearly upset the otherwise brave animal, and the guard was forced to conclude that it was something paranormal in nature. In light of the haunted reputation of the cemetery, he is convinced that it was the spirit of the ghostly lad that spooked his dog that night; no other explanation makes sense to him. Animals, after all, are thought to be more intuitive than human beings when it comes to the supernatural.

Most of the time, encounters with the ghostly child are far more lighthearted than the one reported by that security guard. One that stands out involves a youthful visitor, a boy of about 12 at the time of his visit to Black Creek Pioneer Village, who had a literal run-in with his spectral counterpart. "I was racing along the dirt road near the mill when I bumped into someone I hadn't seen," he told us some five years after the fact. "I bounced backward and landed with a thud on the ground. A boy sat sprawled on the road in front of me. 'Are you OK?' I asked. He nodded as I climbed to my feet. 'I'm really sorry,' I said, feeling embarrassed. The boy smiled. I began to brush the dirt off my legs and shorts. When I looked up again the boy was gone. He disappeared in the blink of an eye. It was the strangest thing. The kid had appeared out of nowhere in front of me, and then disappeared just as fast. There is no way it could have been a real kid."

In another incident, a visitor to the village saw a boy in old-fashioned clothes peek his head out from the Fisherville Church. He waved at her, and when she waved in reply he giggled and ducked back into the church. This happened several more times, until the woman and her family entered the church to explore the historic building. She had expected to find the playful boy inside and was therefore stunned when it was empty. When the woman described the experience and the apparition to a staff member across the road in the manse, the staffer assured her that she was not alone and that other people have had similar encounters. This revelation came as quite a shock; the woman had assumed the young boy was just the child of one of the workers at the village who had come to work with his parent for the day. He looked so real that she never imagined for a second he was a ghost.

A tour guide named Cynthia once had her own game of peek-a-boo with the boy. She was leading her group through the village and was just approaching the church when she noticed a freckle-faced boy with a mop of hair and a broad, gap-toothed smile peeking out from behind a woman at the rear of the group. He was young, perhaps eight or nine, and was wearing 19th-century clothing. Cynthia stopped in front of the church and began to relate its history, but the giggling boy's antics made it increasingly difficult to concentrate on her words. Just as her narrative was coming to an end, the boy peeked out one final time, gave a friendly wave, and then was gone.

In October 2007, the village held its second annual All Hallows Eve event. Lantern-lit ghost tours of haunted buildings were conducted, but the cemetery was not included in the itinerary that year. Apparently the ghost boy took exception to being overlooked because tour or no tour, he decided to make his presence known. After all, why should the other ghosts have all the fun?

Tour guide Catherine Luscombe relates the tale: "At the end of one of my ghostly presentations, someone asked me if there were any other haunted buildings on the site. I mentioned the manse and three other buildings that were not included in the tour, but I forgot to mention the cemetery and the dirt road leading to it. I told my group that they were welcome to explore all the open buildings that evening on their own, and I asked them if they happened to experience anything strange or out of the ordinary to please find me and tell me their story.

"Half an hour later, I was waiting at the ghost tour sign in front of Burwick House for the next tour group to gather when a young couple approached me. They appeared out of breath and somewhat shaken. The young man told me he had a strange experience while walking back from the cemetery on the dirt road. He said he felt a 'persistent pulling and tugging sensation' at the back of his jacket as they walked up the road. He asked his wife if she was grabbing his jacket. His wife told him that she was not touching him at all. The strange sensation continued until they reached the point where the road turns off by the mill. There the pulling and tugging on his jacket stopped altogether. He was very unnerved by what had happened and asked me if I knew of any ghosts in that area. It was then that I told them the story of the ghost boy. He was shocked and nodded in agreement. 'It felt exactly like a child was reaching up and tugging at the back of my jacket, but every time I turned around to look, no one was there.'"

Cemeteries are meant to be sombre places where we grieve and remember lost ones. They can be depressing, lifeless places. And yet, the tiny cemetery at Black Creek Pioneer Village evokes a youthful energy thanks to the cheerful apparition of an undead boy who has made the graveyard his playground. The youngster is too restless to lie within his burial plot. For him, the stream of visitors who pass through everyday represents an inexhaustible supply of new playmates. Why follow the rules and remain at rest after you've died when there's so much fun to be had among the living??

The Simcoe Hotel

Some ghost stories can be easily dismissed as hallucination, misinterpretation or outright fabrication. Others, however, are far more difficult to discount. They are related by sensible people with nothing to gain by falsifying a story and have a foundation of historical fact upon which to stand. Barrie's Simcoe Hotel is the location of one such story. Records indicate it has a very good reason to be haunted, and credible eyewitnesses suggest that a 19th-century tragedy has left a spiritual mark on the building. Here, at one of Barrie's most historic buildings, fact, fantasy and history come together to tease the imagination.

People have sworn they've seen a woman wearing a long dress standing motionless and deathly pale amidst the shadows of the historic building, and that sudden cold breezes without an obvious source can suddenly caress one's face. What these eyewitnesses couldn't possibly have known is that, in the winter of 1872, a woman named Elizabeth Meyer froze to death outside the hotel after a lengthy bout of drinking. They also couldn't have known that this unfortunate woman's frost-shrouded corpse was brought into the hotel to be examined by a coroner and remained therein for a number of days during the subsequent inquest. The deathly woman and chilling breeze experienced by modern-day staff and patrons is almost certainly Elizabeth Meyer making her presence known.

The story of the Simcoe Hotel and its resident haunt begins more than a century ago, at a time when Barrie was a wild and woolly frontier town with numerous taverns and houses of ill repute. In 1853, when there were already six hotels in a town with a population of only 1400, James E. Dunlop came to the unlikely conclusion that Barrie needed at least one more. And so, with visions of riches to be had, he built the James Dunlop Hotel. Two years later, the tavern-keeper and part-time butcher decided to build a newer, more modern hotel adjacent to his current business. When it opened in the spring of 1856, Dunlop called it the Simcoe Hotel.

Because it was located at the east end of the Penetanguishene Road (today Highway 93), the Simcoe Hotel was ideally placed to serve as the principal stopping place in Barrie for the Penetanguishene stage. The thrice weekly service did much to boost Dunlop's wealth, as it brought plenty of overnight guests to his establishment in an era when most hotels survived almost entirely off the proceeds of their bars.

But the hotel also had the misfortune of being located at the Five Points, a rowdy neighbourhood populated by numerous watering holes frequented by local toughs and rugged lumbermen from the lakeshore mills. It was all too common for these inebriated ruffians to stumble into the Simcoe Hotel, buy a bottle of whisky and, after draining it, crack the bottle over the head of an unsuspecting patron. A vicious brawl would invariably ensue, more often than not spilling into the street and ending only when the constable arrived on scene. Through no fault of its owner, the Simcoe Hotel gained notoriety in Barrie.

The reputation only grew after Meyer's tragic and somewhat mysterious death. It was late one January evening in 1872 when Elizabeth Meyer, a woman with a well-known taste for cheap booze, left the warmth of the Simcoe Hotel and stepped out into the cold winter darkness. Wind howled through the town, scrabbling at buildings and cutting through even the thickest layers of clothing. Snow fell steadily from a dark sky. The streets were empty, as usual; unrestrained lawlessness had led many respectable folk to believe the streets were no longer safe at night, and the fierce storm kept most others indoors by the warmth of the hearth. Elizabeth Meyer had no fears about her safety. She had walked these roads countless times without incident, on even the foulest of nights, and no doubt thought this evening would be uneventful as well. Her misplaced confidence would be her undoing.

Pulling her shawl tightly around her neck, Elizabeth waded out into the cold, bound for home. Driving snow stung her face, and the wind whipped her skirts around her legs. She hadn't gone far when a figure emerged from the intense blackness before her. In her drunken haze, she didn't immediately recognize the danger. Then a sharp cry of pain broke from her lips; a meaty fist had slammed into her face, sprawling her upon the frozen road. Drunk only moments before, the intense pain quickly sobered her. But before she could act, her assailant was upon her once again. In the violent confusion, her thoughts turned to the husband she knew she would soon be leaving behind. For a matter of minutes there was only gasping, strangled breathing. Then there was silence.

Early the following morning, a passerby made the horrific discovery of Elizabeth Meyer's body. It was partly obscured by newly fallen snow, limbs frozen in struggle, her twisted features offering no illusions as to the horror she experienced in her final moments. Elizabeth's corpse was brought into the hotel, and it was there that the coroner held his inquest. Incredibly, the death was officially ruled an accident. The coroner suggested that Elizabeth had too much to drink, had passed out in the street outside the hotel, and then simply died of exposure. This explanation was, in the minds of many people, ludicrous. They pointed to the bruises that covered Elizabeth's body—as if she had fallen under a rain of vicious blows—as evidence of murder. They were certain the coroner had made a hasty judgment and that a more thorough inquest was in order. But Elizabeth Meyer was a poor, working class woman and a drunk to boot. Lives like hers were cheap in the 19th century, and so within a matter of days people lost interest in the crime. She faded quickly from the public eye, only to return more than a century later in a manner no one could have anticipated.

In February 1876, a few years after Meyer's death, the Simcoe Hotel was destroyed by fire. Dunlop, uninterested in rebuilding, sold the property to an Irishman named Michael Shanacy. The new hotel Shanacy raised, known as Simcoe House, was a grand structure built entirely of brick and significantly larger than its predecessor. Thankfully, the fire and subtle name change seemed to absolve the business of its notoriety. Under numerous other proprietors, in various guises, and over more than a century of time, the old Simcoe Hotel never again experienced anything like the wild days of the 1860s and '70s.

Its wild past, and even the tragic tale of Elizabeth Meyer, were eventually, for the most part, forgotten.

Today, a newly rejuvenated Simcoe Hotel is far removed from its notorious 19th-century self. After years of existing as an outdated bar with a karaoke stage, the building has been reinvented as a modern restaurant with a casual fine-dining atmosphere. And yet, it seems the Simcoe Hotel cannot escape its past so easily. A fresh coat of paint and new furnishings do little to conceal the fact that the warm and inviting restaurant is haunted by events that occurred in the distant past.

Just ask "Tiffany" (real name changed), who was at one time in the early 2000s a waitress at the Simcoe Hotel. She adamantly asserts that she had several paranormal encounters in the historic building. It was autumn of her first year at the restaurant when Tiffany began to suspect there might be something unusual about her place of employment. She spent the first few months learning the routines and getting to know other staff members, so her focus was firmly on her work during that time. By October, however, she was growing comfortable and becoming familiar with the building. That's when she started to become more aware of her surroundings and suspicious that there is far more to the Simcoe Hotel than meets the eye.

On more than one occasion, Tiffany had the impression that someone or something was following her around. She initially shrugged it off, convincing herself it was only her imagination or perhaps the intent gaze of a male patron, but when she began to feel light touches on her shoulder when no one was within reach, she found it increasingly difficult to dismiss her feelings. As the months passed, the sensation of being followed and touched by an invisible stalker grew in intensity and frequency.

Shortly after Christmas, the escalating paranormal activity took a disturbing new twist. This next experience would be even more difficult to dismiss, since it now involved actually seeing a spirit. Tiffany remembers the night well. It was cold and wet, with snow and sleet falling steadily on gusting winds—eerily reminiscent of the night on which Elizabeth Meyer died. The waitress finished her shift and bundled herself up. She pushed open the door and went out into the biting cold. Head down and buried in the collar of her jacket, Tiffany waded through the snow. Then she looked up and, through eyes watered by wind, saw a woman standing before her, seemingly unaffected by the storm raging around her.

"She looked three-dimensional, like a real person, but she was kind of indistinct. I couldn't make out her features. I didn't think much of it at first, but the woman just stood there frozen to the spot and staring right at me. I remember thinking there was something cold about the look on her face," remembers Tiffany. Unnerved by the woman's strange behaviour, Tiffany looked away for a second. When she looked back, the strange woman had simply disappeared. "But even though I couldn't see her, she was still there. I heard the distinct sound of footsteps crunching through the wet snow to pass by me and head toward the restaurant. I even felt an icy cold chill as the now-invisible woman brushed past me. It was only then that my mind registered that I had seen a ghost."

There were several further incidents after that one, which only added to Tiffany's growing certainty that the Simcoe Hotel was inhabited by an unquiet spirit. One time, the waitress saw a woman wearing a long dress lying stretched out on the floor inside the building. She was motionless and deathly pale, but otherwise looked entirely real. A sudden cold breeze, as if someone had opened a freezer right beside her, caressed Tiffany's face. For a second she considered rushing to the woman's aid, but as the figure faded from sight Tiffany realized the woman was beyond assistance. She was already dead—130 years dead.

When pressed for details about the spirit she had seen twice, Tiffany struggles. "I can't describe many details about her. The events only lasted a couple of seconds each time, but I just sense that she's been gone a very long time and is very sad. Her death was tragic. She's middle-aged but pretty, and she wears a heavy shawl. But it's just a sense, maybe something my mind is creating as a way of giving my feelings some context."

Tiffany isn't the only one to encounter someone from beyond the grave in the Simcoe Hotel, of course. Patrons have occasionally complained of unnatural breezes and deathly cold spots. One man was so startled when a ghostly-white woman suddenly materialized before him that he went into shock. Even after his companions escorted him from the building he could only stare stupidly ahead, his eyes wide in terror, all colour having drained from his face.

A former manager also had an experience. It was late one night, after everyone had left the building and the doors were securely locked, that he saw a woman walking down a hallway. He followed her, thinking that perhaps she had somehow been locked in, but as he drew near the woman simply faded from view. Suddenly, the sound of slow, methodical footsteps came from behind him. He spun around, but he saw no one. By now his heart pounded in his chest like a drum in a hollow cave. Feeling the tide of terror rising and threatening to drown him, he quickly exited the building. He was so convinced that he was not alone in the building that night that he went to the trouble of reviewing security footage the next day. Nothing appeared on film but his ashen face as he futilely searched for the spectral intruder.

Like many ghost stories, those involving the Simcoe Hotel are murmurs and whispers mostly, the type of second-hand rumour that never seems to have a definitive source. But, while these tales might well be embellished and in some cases even entirely fabricated, there does seem to be a historic foundation for them. At Barrie's Simcoe Hotel, fact and fiction are hopelessly intertwined, resulting in a thrilling—and tragic—ghost story.

Sainte-Marie among the Hurons

History is everywhere at Sainte-Marie among the Hurons. It's in the foundations of the original 17th-century Jesuit missionary fort upon which the current buildings have been rebuilt. It's in the relics archaeologists unearthed on site and which are today prominently displayed in the museum. It's in the graves of inhabitants, Jesuit and Huron alike, who were solemnly laid to rest here nearly 400 years ago. And, if whispered stories are to be believed, history also lives in the form of ethereal spirits that lurk within the shadows of the recreated fort, occasionally revealing themselves to remind visitors of the heartaches and troubles that the mission endured during its brief existence.

History comes to life at Sainte-Marie among the Hurons.

The first French settlers had just arrived in New France when the Jesuit priests' zeal to spread the word of God to the Indian nations brought them deep into Canada's wilderness interior. By the 1620s they frequented the large and powerful Huron nation on the shores of Lake Huron, some 1000 kilometres west of the settlement of Quebec. Contact was so frequent and the prospects of converting the Huron deemed favourable enough that within a decade, religious authorities felt they had to have a permanent base there. As a result, in 1639 Jesuit missionaries established a substantial fortified mission in the centre of the Huron domain, which they called Sainte-Marie among the Hurons. From there, several other missions were established nearby.

Despite being located in the midst of dense wilderness hundreds of miles away from the nearest European community in Montreal and surrounded by suspicious, occasionally even hostile natives, the fort quickly prospered and its population grew. Sainte-Marie developed into a remarkably well-fortified compound featuring as many as a dozen structures, some made of stone, all surrounded by sturdy stockades. By 1648, Sainte-Marie was home to more than 60 priests, soldiers and craftsmen, representing one-fifth of the European population of New France.

Although the mission was growing and was proving successful in converting some Huron, troubles were brewing like a dark cloud on the horizon. The French brought influenza, measles and smallpox to the native population, which had no immunity to these foreign bacteria and was consequently ravaged by successive deadly epidemics. It's estimated that the number of Huron was halved within a decade as a result of disease. Clashes of culture between natives and the French, who were blamed for bringing illness with them, grew more intense. And worst of all, traditional animosities between the Huron and the Iroquois to the south were resurfacing. Weakened by disease, the Huron nation was almost powerless to resist when their ancestral enemies invaded.

In July 1648, the Jesuit mission of St. Joseph was destroyed by an Iroquois war band. Father Antoine Daniel, a Jesuit missionary, was killed alongside many Huron. A year later, fathers Jean de Brebeuf and Gabriel Lalemant, along with hundreds of Huron, were captured and killed at the mission of St. Ignace. Rather than await the assault they knew was sure to follow, the inhabitants of Sainte-Marie burned the mission and retreated to St. Joseph's Island (modern-day Christian Island) on Georgian Bay, where they established Sainte-Marie II. But without a friendly population on which to rely for support, this new mission was doomed to failure. After a winter of starvation that saw many deaths, the Jesuits abandoned Sainte-Marie II and, together with a few hundred Christian Huron, left for Quebec. They never returned, and in time the wilderness claimed the fire-blackened ruins of Sainte-Marie.

The story of Sainte-Marie among the Hurons is rich in powerful emotions: faith, courage, horror, despair and fear. If ghosts are born of such emotions as many experts believe they are, then it makes sense that Sainte-Marie should be haunted. Indeed, over the years many people have become convinced that the recreated mission is inhabited by shadows of former residents, pointing to unsettling personal experiences as proof.

The central building in the Sainte-Marie complex is the Church of St. Joseph. Built to accommodate the spiritual needs of the Huron and to inspire those natives curious about Christianity, the church represents Jesuit efforts to bridge the gap between the Huron and French cultures. As a result, within the building one finds Catholic religious trappings wrapped in a symbolism relatable to the Huron; it's a church like no other.

It also represents the resting place of Jean de Brebeuf and Gabriel Lalemant. On March 16, 1649, the two priests were among those captured by attacking Iroquois forces at the village of Saint Louis. The Jesuit martyrs were tortured to death in the most brutal fashion. It's believed that the Iroquois dragged their suffering out over a number of days to better savour the experience, and that the blood-curdling cries of the priests could be heard echoing night and day through the forest. When a Huron counter-attack successfully drove the Iroquois from the region, the French retrieved the remains of the two priests and buried them in the church. Prior to abandoning Sainte-Marie, the Jesuits exhumed the bodies. The bones of Jean de Brebeuf and Gabriel Lalemant were taken as sacred relics, but the flesh of both men was reinterred in a single coffin and buried once more beneath the church floor.

Today, the Church of St. Joseph, where the grave of the martyred saints is found, is said to be full of spiritual energy. Some people report experiencing unusual, even overwhelming emotions while within this building.

Perhaps that's to be expected in a place of such holy gravity. Others claim that photos taken of the grave either fail to develop or reveal glowing orbs that were not visible to the naked eye at the time the photos were taken. Some experiences, blessedly rare, are horrifyingly at odds with the sacred nature of the building.

It wasn't long after entering the church that James realized he was strangely dizzy. At first it was mere light-headedness—perhaps the result of too much sun?—but soon his head was swimming and he felt slightly nauseated. His vision blurred and his hearing became muted. Dimly he perceived a pair of dark shadows peeling off from the wall and gliding silently toward him, and he swore he heard agonizing screams that echoed in his skull. James tried to speak, to call out to his friend, but he couldn't quite find the strength. Instead, he found himself paralyzed, unable to flee from the shadows coming toward him. He was completely at the mercy of the entities now reaching for him with outstretched arms of inky darkness. He closed his terror-filled eyes, unable—unwilling—to watch any longer.

James felt a momentary shudder as something cold touched his chest. He gasped as a chill coursed through his body, seemingly turning the blood in his veins to ice. It was the most intense cold he had ever experienced. A breath or two later, the supernatural chill was gone, melted away. James willed himself to open his eyes a crack, half expecting to find before him a leering shadow ready pounce. But there were no ghosts to be seen—nothing untoward at all. The dizziness had gone as well, and his senses were restored. The whole experience had taken no more than a few seconds, but for James it had felt like a terror-filled eternity.

But despite the spiritual power of the church and its martyrs' grave, some of the most haunting experiences occur in and around the humble cemetery just outside, where 20 Huron and a lone Frenchman (believed to be Jacques Douart, murdered in 1648 by traditional Huron hoping to scare the Jesuits away) are interred.

"As soon as I emerged from the church and the cemetery came into view, I was overcome by sadness for no reason," related Teresa of a visit seven years in the past. "One minute I was enjoying myself, and then I came to the cemetery and I felt despair. I sensed the spirit of a Huron mother grieving for her baby, a baby taken from her by a disease. I could almost see—maybe I did see—the mother clinging to her child, desperate not to let it go, refusing to believe it was dead. The experience shocked me deeply and left me shivering and covered in goose bumps even though it was a hot summer day. I truly believe I tapped into spectral emotions lingering there, perhaps because I am a mother myself and could relate to the torment she suffered from."

Interestingly enough, it was only later, after reading a tourist booklet about Sainte-Marie, that Teresa discovered that the first people buried in the cemetery were a Huron baby and her mother. Cemeteries are a place where families torn apart by death are reunited; in the case of this tragic pair it might be the literal truth. Their story is a heart-achingly sad one, the kind from which ghosts are so frequently spawned.

Winter, 1640. A Huron woman has roused herself from sleep. She wanted nothing more than to remain at rest in the comfort of her bed, warm furs pulled tightly around her body to protect against the morning chill. But she couldn't. Hearing the caw of a crow and seeing a stream of sunlight filtering through the smoke hole in the long-house's roof, she forced herself into motion. Every day, every hour was counting against the infant girl cuddled up against her. The woman wasn't convinced that the village medicine men had the skill to save her child from the mysterious ailment that had her feverish and on the verge of death. The fearful mother knew the odds were stacked against her baby. After all, dozens of villagers, many of them healthy adults, with the same debilitating symptoms had died over the past few months. What chance did her baby have?

The woman knew her child's only hope now lay with the Black Robes and their seemingly magical medicine. Some of her fellow villagers were suspicious of these pale-skinned foreigners who preached of a single god, but she had seen their healing powers and believed—*prayed*—that they could save her baby. It was going to be a long walk to the Black Robes' stockade fort, and before she could set out she would have to carefully spoon broth and water into her child's mouth to keep up her energy for the journey. The wailing baby had been growing slowly weaker, and she worried that if she didn't leave today her child would be too sick to attempt the trip later.

After feeding her child, the woman slipped into fur robes, tucked her baby inside close to her chest and left the longhouse. It was like stepping through the gates of a frozen hell. From the comforting warmth of the long-house she entered a blistering world of bone-chilling cold. Snow covered the landscape in a carpet of white and draped heavily over evergreens, bending them low at the waist. Gusts of icy wind battered against her, and the grey sky above promised more snow again soon. Ignoring the cold, the woman trudged off into the forest, head down against the wind and labouring with each step through deep drifts. She tired but would not stop to rest; her daughter's life hung precariously in the balance, and that knowledge drove her to feats of endurance she didn't think possible.

At last, just as her last strength was failing her, the woman spotted the wooden palisades of Sainte-Marie in the distance. Buoyant now, she found new energy and raced onward. It was only after she handed her child over to the Black Robes and tearfully begged them to help that the Huron woman collapsed in exhaustion. She was beyond tired, but for the first time in days felt a sense of hope. She had faith her daughter could now be saved and allowed herself to slip into a deep sleep.

Unfortunately, her daughter had been beyond help. When she awoke she found herself surrounded by solemn-faced missionaries. She didn't have to be told—she saw the lifeless body of her child lying by her side. As impossible and cruel as it seemed, her baby girl was dead. She sobbed and barely heard the words as the Black Robes gently told her that her daughter was with God now, that there had been nothing they could do to save her. The mother became inconsolable. From that day forth, she refused food and drink. She had made up her mind to die. It was the only way she could be with her beloved baby again.

A psychic who toured the grounds found herself suddenly assaulted by the spirit of the native woman, a spirit who she says has been twisted by the torment of eternal grieving. No longer a beautiful young woman, she is now a hideous figure with tangled hair, wild eyes and a bent back. According to the psychic, this apparition was driven mad by the loss of her only child and fled the beautiful woods and peaceful villages she had once loved to take up residence among the rotting trees and festering pools of the area's most putrid swamps. She ventures out of the wilds only occasionally to return to her daughter's grave and mourn her loss.

But other restless spirits are confined to the Church of St. Joseph and its adjacent cemetery. If one looks hard enough, one can find unusual experiences tied to most of the locations within the palisades of Sainte-Marie. Indeed, the whole grounds may be spiritually charged. One eyewitness, for example, writing on the Toronto Ghosts and Hauntings Research Society message boards, reported hearing an echo of the Sainte-Marie mission as it would have sounded nearly 400 years ago, perhaps in the chaotic moments as the Jesuits evacuated their home of just a decade. "My husband and I heard muffled voices coming from the fort which sounded like hundreds of people gathering there. It was as we were walking by at 3 AM. When I shared my story, others described the same experience," Kathy wrote.

The little cemetery at Sainte-Marie is a reminder of the suffering endured over the decade of the mission's existence.

Susan had an experience of her own at Sainte-Marie in 1997. She was exploring the fort as an interested tourist, hanging on the words of the costumed interpreters and happily soaking up the atmosphere. Ghosts were the furthest thing from her mind. "I was in one of the rooms listening to some history of the building when I felt a strange energy just behind me. It's so hard to describe, but I found myself staring toward the fireplace for no apparent reason. Afterward I asked the tour guide if there was 'anything' in the building. He had noticed me staring at the fireplace, and said that a psychic had been there saying two very angry spirits—an Indian and a Jesuit—were felt there."

The love of a mother is indescribably powerful, but can it survive death? Faith can see us through the most difficult of times, but can it guide us during the transition from the living world to the afterlife? These philosophical questions seem to be answered at Sainte-Marie among the Hurons. Here, bound to a tiny cemetery, the melancholy ghost of a mother mourns the loss of her child, who was pried from her loving embrace by the cruel hands of death. It's also here that a pair of Jesuit priests killed by the Iroquois have been laid to rest—and now return as forlorn spirits.

The ghosts of Sainte-Marie died in situations that evoked extreme emotion, and these emotions have only grown more powerful and intense beyond the grave. As a result, a visit to this important historical site and popular tourist attraction never fails to invoke a response in visitors. Sometimes it's just an appreciation for the past or the hardships endured by the Jesuits and the Huron they ministered to. Other times, however, the response is far more chilling and personal, a reaction to a creepy supernatural encounter with spirits from the past that remain bound to the present.

Sainte-Marie among the Hurons holds the spirits of the dead in its grasp, its wooden palisades keeping them in just as securely as they were meant to keep the enemy out. Who knows when these ghosts might finally scale the walls and pass on to the Great Beyond?

George Stathakis

The building grows dark as, one by one, room by room, lights are turned off for the evening. The young man left behind to shut down the IMAX Theatre finds himself feeling uncomfortable with the sudden darkness. He has heard the stories that circulate among staff about the odd triangular building and the unsettling occurrences that take place in the still of the night, and as he completes his routine the various tales begin to play through his mind. The darkness seems unnaturally tense tonight.

While he's in the gift shop, something unusual catches his eye. Looking down the hall, he sees what almost appears to be a spotlight shining on one of the artifacts in the Daredevil Gallery. There shouldn't be any lights on in that room, the man realizes, hair starting to rise on the back of his neck. He takes a few tentative steps toward the light, intent on investigating, when an agonizing cry shatters the silence, echoing out from the exhibit hall. The scream has barely died when it's replaced by the shiver-inducing sound of fingernails scratching frantically on wood. The young man shakes with fright and finds himself unable to move, frozen to the spot. His mind tells him to get far away from the exhibit as quickly as possible, but as hard as he tries to run, his body refuses to obey.

To his relief, the horrifying scratching quickly fades, the cry never repeats itself and the unnatural light dims. The experience ends as rapidly and inexplicably as it began, leaving the traumatized man to wonder just what happened. Had he encountered the ghost he had heard so much about?

What was behind the haunting? He quit soon after, unwilling to confront the truth. And so the mysteries of the IMAX Theatre are still to be deciphered.

When most people think of the city of Niagara Falls, more often than not what comes to mind is the entertainment district of Clifton Hill. It's the ultimate tourist trap, with wax museums and amusements competing for space alongside over-priced restaurants and gift shops. The lights, the noise and the nonstop mayhem seem garish and gaudy, but seductive and thrilling at the same time. It's difficult to single out one Niagara Falls attraction as the most interesting in town, but the IMAX Theatre must surely rank among the handful of must-sees. And cheerful appearances aside, it's a place with a few haunting mysteries within its walls.

The IMAX Theatre screen is more than six stories high, which is almost overwhelming in terms of visual stimulation. The screen's size, combined with 12,000 watts of digital surround sound, serves to immerse viewers in the film unfolding before them, making them feel as if they are actually a part of the cinematic events. The featured film, *Niagara: Miracles, Myths, and Magic,* tells the story of Niagara Falls in broad strokes, providing tourists who are unfamiliar with the area and its history with a greater appreciation of this natural wonder. The recreation of such timeless spectacles as the Great Blondin's tightrope antics above the gorge and Annie Taylor's plunge over the falls in a barrel makes for gripping viewing. The theatre also houses a National Geographic Store (the only one of its kind in Canada) and the world's largest collection of original daredevil barrels and other related historical artifacts in the Niagara Falls Daredevil Gallery.

This is the side of the IMAX Theatre seen by tourists. But there is another side as well, one that few people are aware of, a side that only reveals itself after dark when the crowds have left and the building becomes eerily empty and silent. This is the time when a ghost emerges to prowl the halls and startle unsuspecting staff members. There's little doubt about the identity of this spirit. Without hesitating, and whether they believe in the supernatural or not, staff identify the spirit as "George," referring to the ill-fated stuntman George Stathakis.

On Saturday, July 5, 1930, George Stathakis, a 46-year-old part-time chef, self-styled mystic and philosopher, and would-be author, went over the falls in a reinforced wooden barrel in search of enlightenment and truth. Stathakis never found what he was looking for. Instead, he suffocated when his barrel failed to surface and remained submerged at the foot of the falls for 18 hours. Stathakis became the second person to perish while attempting to go over the Horseshoe Falls.

Before that fateful day when he assured himself a place in the history books with his ill-starred act of daredevilry, George Stathakis was an obscure man of little consequence. Although records indicate that he was born in Greece in 1884, he sincerely believed he was actually born in central Africa a thousand years earlier on the banks of a mythical river called Abraham. At some point in his early life, Stathakis began to hear disembodied voices and experience strange visions he chalked up to divine inspiration.

It was after this development that he began to create a complex philosophy that blended religion, mysticism and fabrication.

Stathakis was seduced by his fabricated world and fell deeper and deeper into its fold. He became so immersed in his mythical beliefs that he found it increasingly difficult to keep a job or maintain relationships. He was only occasionally employed in a low-wage job as a chef, and his only real friend was a turtle named Sonny Boy. Sonny Boy was no mere pet; Stathakis claimed the turtle was more than 105 years old and was sacred to some obscure Greek cult, the earthly incarnation of a mysterious god-like entity.

Stathakis' version of his life and his philosophical beliefs is laid out in a book he wrote entitled *The Mysterious Veil of Humanity Through the Ages*. Much of the book consists of the mystic supposedly interviewing the great Greek philosophers Aristotle and Plato, both of whom have been dead more than 2000 years. Interestingly enough, he also wrote that he had visited Niagara Falls in the distant past, "at a time when they had not yet been formed."

Clearly, Stathakis was slowly losing his tenuous grip on reality. Further evidence of the delusions clouding his mind was his firm belief that in some distant past he had been the first person to stand at the North Pole, where he had proclaimed himself "king and master of the Earth and from this summit I am going to rule and direct it."

When 1930 rolled around, the increasingly eccentric mystic felt confident he was ready to cross the final threshold into a world beyond our normal understanding.

To do this, he would need to take a leap of faith—quite literally, as it turned out. Stathakis decided he would go over Niagara Falls in a barrel. He was sure the experience would provide mystical insight, and that by staring death in the face he would somehow make a connection with a realm of consciousness otherwise only witnessed when we leave this mortal existence upon death. Stathakis had another motive as well, intending to sell the motion picture rights to his act of daredevilry to finance a three-volume book series detailing the secret history of humankind from its origins to the far future.

On July 5, 1930, the 46-year-old and his pet turtle were secured in a custom-made barrel bobbing in the waters of the Niagara River. The barrel was released at 3:25 PM and began racing through the white-capped waters, rising and falling with each wave, hurtling at breakneck speed past thousands of breathless onlookers. Minutes later the barrel disappeared over the falls. It would be 18 hours before it re-emerged. During that long, agonizing period, it was trapped behind the thundering falls. By the time the barrel appeared early the next morning, the few remaining onlookers knew there would be no triumphant emergence of the mystic daredevil. When would-be rescuers pried the barrel's lid off they found Stathakis dead as expected, his face twisted by terror, eyes wide and searching, hands frozen like talons having spent his final moments desperately clawing at the barrel in search of escape—it must have been a terrifying way to go. They were surprised, however, to find Sonny Boy alive and unharmed by the experience. Stathakis would have surely suggested the turtle's survival was evidence of its divinity.

In light of his esoteric beliefs and passionate interest in the afterlife, the tragic nature of his death and the humiliation of being buried in a pauper's grave unmourned by either friends or family, Stathakis makes as likely a choice as any to return from beyond the grave. But why would he choose the IMAX Theatre as his haunt, a building built more than four decades after his demise? The reason lies within the Daredevil Gallery. There, standing unassumingly in the corner, is the red and blue barrel in which Stathakis plunged over the falls and into infamy. At first glance, there is little to set this barrel apart from the others in the museum. It's far from being the most exotic artifact in the collection, but what people don't always appreciate is that for at least 15 hours after his supply of air had been exhausted, this metal-and-wood construct became Stathakis' tomb.

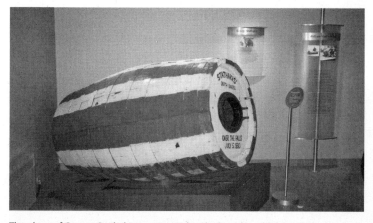

The ghost of George Stathakis remains tied to the barrel in which he died.

It's hard to imagine what horrors the ill-fated daredevil endured while trapped within the barrel's claustrophobic confines. With impenetrable darkness surrounding him and the roar of falling water drowning out all other sounds, his mind must have slowly unravelled. Did he claw furiously at the wood before suffocating, or shout desperately in the vain hope that someone could hear? Did he experience fear or regret, or was he at peace with his end? We can't know for sure. But when the would-be rescuers eventually pulled his lifeless corpse from the barrel, George's glassy, dead eyes stared up at them accusingly, as if to ask, "Why didn't you come sooner?"

Perhaps his final tortured thoughts of betrayal and overwhelming terror are what cause George's spirit to remain tied to the barrel and consequently to the IMAX Theatre, but despite the horrible way in which he died, George seems to be a mischievous entity without malice or remorse. He takes pleasure in knocking items off shelves in the National Geographic Store, or rearranging newly made displays during the night so that when staff return in the morning they have to redo their work. George sometimes plays pranks upon those who find themselves alone in the projection room by making odd noises that have no identifiable source. One projectionist we spoke to noted that he often felt uneasy in the darkened room, as if there was an unseen presence lurking somewhere nearby. Once, he thought he saw someone in the room with him. Maybe a coworker, he thought to himself, though he hadn't seen the door open nor had any light spilled into the room. When he came around the projector to get a closer look, the figure had mysteriously melted into the shadows and was gone from sight.

Paranormal activity at the IMAX Theatre always occurs at night, when the building is darkened and nearly empty. Staff members occasionally hear faint footfalls ascending the projection room stairs or making their way across the Daredevil Gallery. When they investigate, they find themselves alone. Sometimes, when the theatre is especially quiet, rapping can be heard coming from the barrel, as if someone trapped within is signalling for help that can never arrive. Those who are sensitive to such things claim the barrel is heavy with negative energy, as if a part of George has never left. His spirit, they believe, has been ingrained into the wood by the horror of his final moments.

It's possible that George is trying to communicate with us. Before he climbed into the barrel that day in 1930, the mystic assured gathered witnesses that should he perish, his faithful companion, Sonny, would one day reveal the secrets surrounding his stunt. Sonny never uttered a single word, so it's possible George is attempting to do what he entrusted to his turtle. Perhaps the fact that his spirit is still active proves that he found spiritual enlightenment before dying, or that his quest is ongoing and unfulfilled.

One particular staff member's experience seems to support the theory that George Stathakis is attempting to speak from beyond the grave. While working late one night, this individual claims to have heard a voice carrying out from the Daredevil Gallery. There shouldn't have been anyone in the building at the time, so he went to investigate.

The man felt oddly apprehensive and was unsure what he would find. Anxiety caused him to move slowly and quietly, cautiously creeping closer to the exhibit hall. The closer he got the more distinct the voice became, but he couldn't make out what was being said because the words seemed to be in a foreign tongue. By now he was afraid and briefly considered simply leaving the theatre and locking the doors behind him. The part of him that was curious won the internal struggle, however, and after mustering his courage he pressed on. To his surprise, when he entered the Daredevil Gallery he found the hall empty. The mysterious voice, so clear moments ago, was silent. *Must be George acting up*, the relieved man thought to himself before leaving the deceased daredevil to his mystic ramblings.

"George is a peaceful spirit, though I think sad," said then theatre director Elaine Bald, interviewed in 2006. "I've never experienced anything, but many of our staff certainly have and we have no doubt the spirit is that of George Stathakis. Maybe it's natural that we have a ghost or two within the building; the theatre is a pyramid, after all, and many cultures associate the pyramid with mysticism and supernatural power. Certainly George would have believed that to be the case."

Heritage Homestead

While you're seated in a car speeding by, this historic structure looks no different than any number of 19th-century farmhouses found alongside the rural roadways of Simcoe County, Ontario. But there's much more to the building than first meets the eye.

Heritage Homestead, located on Highway 11 at the 5th line of Oro Township, is appropriately named. Nestled in a rural setting, surrounded by rolling fields and groves of trees, this fine example of Victorian architecture gives the overall impression of being rooted firmly in a bygone age, its brick walls untouched by time. That's exactly how the owners of this elegant home décor store, Wendy and Dave Barrer, like it. They worked hard to preserve the look and character of the charming building even while transforming it into a modern retail space where fine furniture, artwork and other decorative pieces are sold. They consider themselves caretakers of the building; they are fully aware that though they own the property today, it will always belong in a spiritual sense to its builder, James A. Ross.

Indeed, many people believe that Ross continues to preside over his former home a century after his death, seemingly unaware that it is no longer his private sanctuary. Rumours of hauntings have surrounded the home for decades but seem to have increased since it was transformed into a retail space, perhaps because of the sheer number of people passing through on a daily basis. At least the stories of paranormal activity are benign in nature, suggesting Ross is content with the manner in which his home has been maintained.

James Ross was born in Kingston in 1837, and in 1858 he married Euphemia Pringle. Six years later they settled into a log house at Oro Station on land that had originally belonged to Euphemia's maternal grandfather, Andrew Masson. James and Euphemia embraced the farm; for them, it represented a bright start to a life together, and they saw in its rich soil all their dreams and aspirations. They named the property New Hope Farm.

The spirit of James A. Ross continues to preside over his former home.

It wasn't long before their hard work transformed the land into a thriving farm with fields of golden wheat, bountiful orchards and a herd of dairy cattle. James also opened a farm equipment store in Barrie. The business was a success and was even mentioned in the September 1, 1888, edition of the *Toronto World* newspaper. "Mr. J. A Ross is an implement agent of experience," the paper reported. "He has a well-stocked store on Dunlop Street [143 Dunlop], which contains all the latest improved machinery that the farmer requires for the successful working of his farm."

The success of the store made Ross a wealthy man and a respected figure. He took advantage of his prominence and began a career in politics, which started in 1877 when he was first elected to council. He rose to become a longtime reeve of Oro Township, and in 1895 he served as warden of Simcoe County.

In 1888, Ross began building a new home more in keeping with his status as an important elected official and a wealthy businessman, large enough to house his nine children. The result was extravagant, with two drawing rooms, six bedrooms, a formal dining room, a birthing room off the kitchen and a carriage house. The downstairs boasted 12-foot-high ceilings, while a sweeping oak staircase led to the lavishly furnished rooms upstairs. In all, some 92,000 bricks were used in the construction, all of which had to be brought from a Barrie brickyard by horse and wagon.

James Ross loved his home, and he enjoyed many happy moments with his family there. Perhaps that's why some people believe that after his death in 1917, his spirit returned there and has never left. With so many fond memories tied to his beloved house, a building that reflected all the success his hard work provided, is it any wonder he refuses to let go?

Wendy and Dave Barrer can easily understand how someone could have such a strong emotional attachment to a building, and in particular to this one. They've experienced the feeling themselves. "We visited the building years before we bought it, back when it was an art gallery called Decorator's Gallery. I remember standing on the porch with snowflakes coming down around me and saying to my husband, 'One day we'll own this home.' I don't know why or how, but somehow I sensed it. I just knew we were destined to own it," Wendy recalls.

The Barrers took possession in 2001 and opened Heritage Homestead in April 2002. It wasn't long before they began to suspect that they shared the building with an otherworldly resident. When they bought the place, Wendy naturally wanted to give it a facelift inside—a fresh look for a fresh start. Worn carpets were ripped out. Paint was touched up. The old wallpaper was removed and replaced with almost an exact match that was painstakingly tracked down.

"As part of the renovation process we took digital measurements of every room and hallway, for insurance purposes and so forth," Wendy says, reflecting on warm memories. "We didn't have any problems until we came to the staircase. For some reason we couldn't get a reading of it, and we tried several times. The machine just wouldn't work there. It was puzzling." Wendy and Dave had no explanation. The digital measuring device was functioning perfectly fine moments before, and it began working again minutes later when used in other areas of the house. It just wouldn't work in that one location.

The staircase has since become associated with other paranormal activity. Wendy reports that occasionally they will smell the lingering odour of cigar smoke in the stairway and that some of their sensitive customers feel spiritual activity is strongest there.

The staircase at Heritage Homestead is a hot spot for paranormal activity.

One psychic customer had a particularly strong and memorable experience at Heritage Homestead. She generously shared her unique insight. "Walking into the magnificent building gave me warm feelings," she began, eyes closed in concentration. "Images of past events flashed through my mind: the laughter of children running up and down the staircase as dad shouts for them to be careful; mom, meanwhile, lovingly creates another delicious meal in the kitchen while occasionally looking in on the newest addition to the family, a rosy-cheeked baby who quietly naps in the adjoining birthing room. They're just images without context, but I go with my feelings. Somehow I know this was a very loving family. But sadly, I also sensed that tragedy struck them as they lost one of their own. When I walked into the kitchen and birthing room, I instantly got the lingering emotion of this great loss, and I felt the sadness of a mother with a broken heart."

Research uncovered that James and Euphemia Ross did indeed lose a child in infancy, a child who may well have died in the birthing room. Was this the loss that the psychic sensed? It certainly fits.

"I heard the pitter-patter of small feet running upstairs, perhaps playing hide-and-seek, and I sensed the father chuckling in amusement at the antics of his children," the psychic continued as memories flooded back to her. "The gentleman enjoyed his daily routine, but nothing brought him more pleasure than coming home to his wife and kids. It's a very comforting sensation."

The strength of his love for his family would explain why James Ross chooses to stay in his former house.

Those four walls contain a lifetime of fond memories, and the building represents a tangible link to the family from whom his earthbound spirit is separated.

Although Wendy Barrer notes that no one in the family has yet seen a shadowy figure roaming from room to room, she is quick to point out that when her children were younger they sensed the presence of a spirit. "They were adamant there was an invisible male figure in the house with us. It faded as they got older, and I understand that is supposed to happen; children are able to pick up on the paranormal stronger than adults can. I wouldn't discount the possibility of ghosts, though I've never seen one or had a frightening experience. If we have a ghost, he's never bothered me or made me nervous."

The same can't be said for staff and customers, several of whom swear to have had unusual experiences and unsettling feelings—a sense of an unseen presence, inexplicable sounds, the occasional whisper or disembodied footstep from an adjacent room. But regardless of whether or not they believe in ghosts, most visitors agree this building has a definite spirit to it.

"I always thought the house liked us, and we tried to maintain its unique character—inviting, warm, friendly," says Wendy. "We feel we're caretakers of this beautiful old home and the history it represents. I hope that makes the spirit happy."

Ghosts of Ballycroy

The term ghost town is often misconstrued. People imagine a derelict village with a paranormal population, ruined buildings inhabited by ghostly residents. In truth, a ghost town is simply a community that is but a shadow of its former self, often completely abandoned, but sometimes with a handful of flesh-and-blood people living alongside decaying homes, overgrown cemeteries and empty lots.

Once in a while, however, the ghost town of imagination meets that of reality. Here, one never knows if the front door of that abandoned home is swinging open on the wind or whether an unseen entity is ushering you inside; it's hard to know if the mournful groan you hear is the wind stalking you through the woods or a restless soul; and the buzzing, bloated flies gathering by the dozen on that grimy window may be perfectly natural, but they might also hint at something sinister at work. Ballycroy is one such ghost town, an atmospheric ruin of a community where the supernatural is most definitely a fact of life.

Located about an hour north of Toronto, Ballycroy has changed greatly since the days when horses struggled to pull heavily laden wagons along its rutted roads and when logs were felled by the hundreds to feed the insatiable appetite of the local mills. Back then it was a thriving village, home to a dozen businesses and several hundred people who looked to the future with optimism. Now most of the buildings have long since been reclaimed by the forest or ravaged by time, the population has been reduced to a mere handful, and the dreams and aspirations of previous inhabitants lie shattered in the foundation holes that litter the area.

By 1810, settlers were already expanding out of Toronto into the surrounding counties, pushing the network of roads farther into the wilderness. When two major roads intersected, a village of some importance naturally arose. Ballycroy straddled the road north from Toronto and one east from Orangeville. The first settler to arrive was Samuel Beatty, who established a sawmill on the nearby Humber River in 1819. Other settlers began to arrive soon after Beatty established his mill, most of whom were Irishmen who named the growing village after a town in their homeland. In time, the community prospered, boasting a population of 400 citizens and more than a dozen businesses. People looked to the future with enthusiasm, sure that great things were in store for Ballycroy. Unfortunately, their confidence was misplaced.

Ballycroy lasted less than a century. A devastating fire in 1875 destroyed several businesses, while others began to shift to Palgrave and Alliston, both of which, unlike Ballycroy, had recently been reached by the railway. From a peak population approaching 400 in 1875, the town dwindled to 200 souls in 1881 and a mere 150 by 1900. What turned the sleepy hamlet into a virtual ghost town was the straightening of the Orangeville road (Highway 9) and the Toronto-north road (Highway 50) in the early 20th century so as to bypass Ballycroy entirely.

Today, Ballycroy is a tranquil shadow of its former boisterous glory. To see it now, it's hard to believe this community was once thriving. Opposite a false-fronted general store, recently rebuilt into a handsome residence, stands a weathered sign announcing Ballycroy. The old Orangeville road, now overgrown by weeds, runs off into the woods. Alongside this forlorn path are numerous foundations and a lone surviving home, boarded up and strangely ominous, standing partially obscured by a veil of trees.

In Ballycroy, the echoes of those who lived and died in the village can still be heard amongst the trees, along the empty streets and in the foundation holes. Could these echoes be real, the spirits of former villagers who have been unable to pass on to the afterlife and remain trapped in their former homesteads? Ghosts have been known to suddenly materialize before startled witnesses and then melt back, just as suddenly, into the silent shadows. Ballycroy, it seems, is not merely an abandoned village, but a real ghost town, one where souls from the past float soundlessly along overgrown roads and tenaciously cling to their former homes.

The Victorian Lady

One of the few original buildings to remain in Ballycroy is the former McClelland general store and hotel, now lovingly restored as a private residence. The historic, handsome, two storey structure is home to another a relic of a bygone era, an elderly woman from the past who stubbornly refuses to pass on to the other side.

Longtime Ballycroy resident and self-proclaimed town historian Dave Bond related the tale to us. "Do you know about our resident ghost?" he asked, clearly hoping we had not so he could regale us with the story. "She's an old lady who inhabits the hotel. She's harmless but has startled people when she suddenly appears out of thin air."

Some time ago, according to Bond, after the building had ceased to function as a store and hotel, an elderly woman was a guest of the family residing there. She was the mother of one of the inhabitants, as Bond recalls, but he doesn't remember whether it was the husband or wife. Either way, the woman slept in one of the upstairs rooms and thought it was something of a thrill to be staying in a room that hotel guests would have booked into in years past. The room was even furnished with Victorian charm: the bed had an ornate brass headboard, the nightstand was of aged wood and probably handcrafted, and a hook rug lay across the well-worn floorboards.

One night, hours after she had settled into bed with a thick quilt pulled up around her shoulders, the woman awoke to the feeling of a presence in the room. She sensed a pair of eyes piercing into her from somewhere in the darkness. When her eyes adjusted to the gloom, the woman saw another old lady, bony and thin, dressed in Victorian clothes and with her grey hair in a style long out of date, staring at her as she lay in bed. The frail woman moved toward the bed. The shocked houseguest noted that the floorboards, which normally groaned wearily whenever someone walked upon them, made no noise of protest as her mysterious visitor moved closer. She then noticed that the approaching figure wasn't actually walking but rather floating, her legs coiling and roiling like wisps of smoke caught in a gentle breeze. Mouth dry, a slight tremor of fear quivering her lips, the woman knew she was seeing a ghost.

The spirit came to a stop against the bed and looked down at the woman with empty, lifeless eyes. The two stared at one another for several long moments before the ghost finally spoke a single sentence in a hollow voice: "Why are you in my room?"

Before the elderly houseguest could respond, the spirit faded into the darkness and was gone. The entire experience had lasted only a few seconds, but the woman was sure of what she had seen. Although she wasn't frightened, she was naturally startled; she struggled to fall back to sleep and spent the remainder of the night restlessly in the bed.

When morning came and sunlight chased away the shadows, the woman slipped on a robe and went downstairs to speak with her hosts. Over breakfast, she told them about the ghostly encounter, relaying the event in a matter-of-fact manner. They were shocked at how casually she had taken it all, convinced that had they seen the ghost they wouldn't be nearly so calm. But the old woman assured them she was never frightened by the experience. "I'm 90 years old," she said over a cup of steaming coffee. "What could the ghost have done to me?"

A Victorian lady refuses to check out of this former hotel.

Bond shrugs his shoulders. "I haven't seen the ghost, but over the years others have, and I believe them. After all, they have nothing to gain by lying," he says. "It's believed she lived in the hotel at one time during the pioneer era and grew so attached to the building that she wants to continue living there. She doesn't seem to know that she's dead and that her room isn't hers any longer."

Is the ghost that of a former resident, and is an unusually strong affinity for the building the cause of the haunting, as Dave Bond suggests? Or is it some forgotten tragedy that causes this woman, whoever she might be, to remain in the building all these decades later? We'll likely never know. In fact, we don't even know if she is still there. A young couple has recently moved into the old McClelland Hotel and, as of 2010, the aged spectre has yet to make her presence known to the new homeowners. Maybe the tired old woman has finally grown weary of clinging to her old life and has left the hotel behind for a new home on the other side. Only time, which seems to have no meaning in Ballycroy, will tell.

Ghostly Milliners

Peter Small was an ambitious man. He had grand visions and planned to establish a business empire in the village of Ballycroy. The first step toward fulfilling his lofty goal came during the 1850s when Small, still a young man barely in his twenties, built a hotel alongside the village's busy intersection to cater to travellers and stage-coaches. The hotel was known as a fine establishment, and its annual January Ball attracted people from as far away as Toronto to enjoy its revelry. But Small and his clientele were Protestants in what was a Catholic stronghold, and brawls broke out with regularity. A rival innkeeper named James Feheley, who operated a hotel directly across the road, regularly led drunken Catholic patrons in assaulting any lone Protestant leaving Small's inn. Despite this animosity, Peter Small's establishment was a popular stopping point for weary travellers, and he prospered.

Within a decade the hotelier had added a general store with a post office, as well as a woollen goods factory to his holdings. There was little doubt that Peter Small was the wealthiest man in town, and he was buoyant with his rapid success. He was certain great things were in store for himself and for the village he called home. Unfortunately, simmering tensions in Ballycroy were about to bubble over, with tragic consequences.

The night of April 29, 1875, was dark and still. Villagers were tucked soundly into their beds when suddenly the quiet was interrupted by calls of alarm—bright red flames pierced the blackness. Small's hotel was ablaze, the fire hungrily licking at its walls and climbing rapidly toward the roof. Villagers rushed from their beds to fight the inferno, but by the time they arrived there was precious little hope of saving the building. Flames could be seen racing through the halls and engulfing entire rooms in mere minutes. Buckets of water were drawn from a nearby well, but it was a futile gesture.

Suddenly, the villagers saw them: framed by the orange glow of flames were three young women desperately fighting to open a second storey window and reach safety. These women, hardworking, kind and cheerful, were employed as milliners in Small's wool factory and lived at the hotel. They now found themselves trapped by the racing flames. They had tried to flee down the hall but were turned back by hellish heat and blinding smoke. The window was their last hope for escape. The woman fought against the window, first struggling with the latch and then pounding against the thick glass with their hands. In mere moments, however, the flames were upon them. Faces twisted by agony and fright, they died horrible deaths as the fire enveloped their bodies. Watching the women die before their eyes was a sight few in Ballycroy would ever forget, and the gut-wrenching sounds of their final agonizing screams echoed painfully in their memories even decades later.

When dawn finally arrived and the fire had been reduced to smoldering embers, the village took stock of its losses. All told, the raging inferno had claimed the hotel, three residences, a blacksmith shop, McMaster's tavern and a carpenter's workshop. The milliners were the only casualties of the night, but they were enough. As the charred corpses were pulled from the ashes, men and women alike sobbed uncontrollably. The entire community went into a state of shock, then mourning.

Rumours flew fast and furious that the fire had been deliberately set. A second, eerily similar fire that occurred only two months later in Peter Small's temporary residence only confirmed the suspicion of arson in most people's minds. That blaze drove the frightened and despondent man from town for good; he took the fires to be a grim warning and fled to Toronto, never looking back. There was a $5000 reward for the conviction of the arsonist responsible for the fires, and George C. Hughes, editor of the *Cardwell Sentinel*, wrote, "if he [the culprit] be found, Judge Lynch will adjudicate, and hell contains no corner hot enough for him thereafter." Everyone in the area was so enraged by the tragic deaths of the milliners that had the arsonist been found he would undoubtedly have been strung up from a tree by his neck, and few people would have complained.

In the aftermath of the tragedy, the grieving village raised a headstone in memory of the deceased in the cemetery at St. James' Church, four miles to the north. It reads in part: "To the memories of Mary A. Fanning, aged 32 years. Margaret H. Daley, aged 24 years. And Bridget Burke, aged 28 years. Who perished in the conflagration which on April 29, 1875 destroyed the village of Ballycroy, this monument is erected by their afflicted relatives..."

The headstone was the villagers' way of putting their grief to rest. But according to legend, rest was something that the three milliners could not find. The ghosts of Mary Fanning, Margaret Daley and Bridget Burke began to haunt the site of their deaths, and some people claim that a dark ambiance surrounds the sight of the former hotel. The spirits are said to wander the area singly, rather than together. As one would expect, they are troubled souls, tormented by the agonizing pain they endured in their final moments and the tragedy of lives cut far too short. Their presence, it is said, is often preceded by the aroma of smoke and a patch of great warmth, supernatural echoes of the fire that claimed them.

An eyewitness who shared her brief encounter almost 30 years after it happened reported seeing a skirt swish by and then disappear seconds later behind some trees and shrubs. Even though it was from across the road and the sighting lasted perhaps two heartbeats, the woman was certain of what she saw. More to the point, she knew she couldn't have seen a flesh-and-blood person because the woods into which the skirt had disappeared simply weren't thick enough to mask a person. The mysterious skirt-wearing figure had simply vanished. What adds an aura of authenticity to this encounter is the fact that the eyewitness indicated that the ghost had manifested on the exact spot where Small's hotel once stood. While the ghost story of the milliners may be a part of local lore, very few people have such obscure knowledge as the former location of the hotel to be able to fabricate such a tale.

Intriguingly, there is a connection between the haunting of Small's fire-razed hotel and perhaps Canada's most famous ghost story, that of the Black Donnellys of Lucan, Ontario. The seven Donnelly brothers were bullies with a strong hatred of Protestants and a long list of assaults—and murders—to their credit. Yet no one would arrest them, so frightful was their reputation. Their deprecations ended when, on the night of February 3, 1881, an armed band of 35 vigilantes descended upon the Donnelly farmstead and killed five members of the family. The Black Donnellys haunt the farm to this day.

TO
THE MEMORIES OF
MARY A. FANNING
AGED 32 YEARS.

MARGARET H. DALEY
AGED 24 YEARS.

AND BRIDGET BURKE
AGED 28 YEARS.

WHO PERISHED IN THE CONFLAGR-
ATION WHICH ON APRIL 29, 1875:

THIS MONUMENT IS RAISED BY THEIR
AFFLICTED RELATIVES IN GRATEFUL
RECOLLECTION OF THEIR ESTIMABLE
QUALITIES AND EARLY LIVES.

Their departure was taken for misery,
with their going away from us for utter
destruction, but they are in peace and
though in the sight of man they suffer
in torment, their hope is full of immo-
rtality.

R.I.P.

We have buried them in the silent earth, where the birds a requiem sung
We have made them a grave in the field of the dead where the bees their shadows flung
At the foot of the cross, well mourn our loss and weep for their early doom
And pray for the rest of the young and best who died and died so soon.

The three women who died so horribly continue to haunt the site of their demise.

It's well known that the Donnellys were close friends of James Feheley, and that they occasionally visited Ballycroy for some rowdy fun. Perhaps inevitably, suspicion for the fire that destroyed Small's hotel fell upon their shoulders; several of the brood were in the vicinity around the time of the fire. Arson certainly wouldn't have been out of character for the thugs.

Regardless of the cause of the fire, since that terrible night in 1875, bad luck has plagued the village. A cascade of ill fortune conspired to make Ballycroy a ghost town less than a quarter of a century later. Besides vague foundations through which shrubs and trees grow, the occasional appearance of the spectral milliners is the only reminder of Peter Small's hotel. It's not likely the ambitious entrepreneur had such a legacy in mind when he opened the inn back in the mid-19th century.

The Forlorn Cottage

It seems likely that both tragedy and an unusually strong affinity may be responsible for tying Ballycroy's final ghost to his haunt. The original road west from Ballycroy to the town of Orangeville is now little more than an overgrown laneway. After a brief walk, however, the shadowy form of a lone cabin suddenly appears between the dark pines. There's something oddly unsettling about this cabin, almost as if it has purposefully hidden itself away from civilization and resents being intruded upon. It sags with the weight of the ages, the wood weathered grey and rotting. The cottage's windows have all been boarded up with thick plywood; under a moody grey sky or in the failing light of dusk, an overactive imagination might cause one to wonder whether the windows were boarded to keep intruders out or to imprison whatever unspeakable things that make their home within.

Although oppressive today, its origins are decidedly normal. Dave Bond informed us that the cottage was the homestead of the Pettit family, headed by John and Margaret. They were simple farmers, unassuming and humble, the kind of folks one would like to think only good things happen to. They worked the land, raised children, attended church and asked for nothing. Surely good fortune should have been theirs. Fate doesn't always follow such logic. Records show that the Pettit family suffered a terrible tragedy in 1917, a tragedy that may stain their home to this day.

The First World War brought the Pettits pain and loss, as the conflict did for so many families. In 1916, Chester Pettit, who grew up in the tiny three-room cabin, enlisted in the Canadian Army and was promptly shipped to France for front-line duty. He never returned home; Chester Pettit died in the mud, barbed wire and shell holes of Vimy Ridge in 1917. The pathetic remnants of his personal effects and family photos lay with his broken and bloodied body. Undoubtedly, his final thoughts were of home and the loved ones he would never again see.

Or did Chester in fact return home to his family, in spirit if not in body? Some people, these authors included, have come away believing that his spirit haunts the abandoned and derelict Pettit cabin to this day.

We visited Ballycroy almost 90 years after Chester's death in preparation for an article detailing the history of the vanished village, never anticipating the intimate connection we would make with the past. It was early spring, and despite the crystal blue sky and warm sun above, patches of snow stubbornly lingered here and there in the shade. Leaving the car behind, we began to walk into the bush along what was once the road to Orangeville. The ground was still hard with frost, making it difficult to walk; it felt like the distance travelled was measured in years instead of kilometres. We noticed that curbing from the original road could be seen through the tall brown grass, and we were thrilled to discover several foundation holes along the route.

Perhaps the ghost of Chester Pettit is responsible for the oppressive atmosphere that surrounds this cottage.

We had walked perhaps a kilometre or two when we stopped suddenly. Neither of us could believe our eyes: there, looming amidst a copse of skeletal trees, was a forlorn cottage, its windows and doors boarded up, its walls weathered and weary, but still standing and in sound condition.

Feeling an irresistible urge to enter, we climbed through the lone un-boarded window and immediately noticed an overwhelming musty smell. The stink was repellent and hung in the air with the unsettled dust our entrance had kicked up. No one had been here for a long time; that much was immediately obvious.

With only a hint of sunlight filtering in, it was difficult to see so we proceeded cautiously. In the dimness we noted how small the rooms were and that several belongings including steel-frame beds, a lumpy mattress, an old kitchen stove and countless rusted tin cans remained littered about. Filled with excitement, I didn't notice that Maria had started to become uneasy. I wouldn't learn until much later that she had somehow felt we had overstayed our welcome in the little cottage. She instinctively sensed that something was upset that we had intruded upon its solace and wanted us gone, and she knew it was unwise to linger any longer than we already had.

We climbed out through the window, jumped to the ground and retraced our steps back to the car. Maria was unusually silent throughout the walk. I chalked it up to her merely savouring the fine spring day and enjoying the tranquility of the woods. Little did I know that her silence was a result of struggling with the weight of the unnerving experience she had just endured. Before we hopped into the car, I decided to take some last photographs to remember our day of exploration. I took a few of the false-fronted general store, and then I took one final photo of the faded sign announcing Ballycroy.

A few days later, the photos were developed and I noticed something unusual: the image of the sign was unnaturally dark, much more so than those taken just minutes earlier. It was almost sepia-toned. The grey starkness of the photo was in direct contrast to the bright, cloudless day we remembered. Perplexed, I made an offhand comment to Maria, something to the effect of, "It's almost as though someone didn't want us to take this picture."

I may have been more right than I knew. Maria immediately noticed the spectral figure of a man standing behind the sign, and once it was pointed out I agreed the image was unmistakable. Others we showed the photo to also saw the shape without any prompting—even those who didn't believe in the existence of ghosts. That's when Maria opened up and shared her experience within the derelict Pettit cottage. We wondered whether a spectral denizen of the cabin had followed us back to our car. The thought was admittedly a bit disturbing. More chilling was her description of the entity she had sensed in the building: tall with broad shoulders, dark hair, aged early to mid thirties. This, our research would later show, matched the surviving photographs of Chester Pettit almost perfectly.

Had we inadvertently disturbed Pettit by trespassing in his domain? It was almost unbelievable: the uncanny coincidences, the strange happenings, the inexplicable feelings. We were shocked, excited and a little frightened at the same time. To write about ghosts is one thing; to experience them is something else altogether. Now one of the stories of Ballycroy belongs to us.

Removed from the advance of civilization and surrounded by land with an almost timeless feel to it, Ballycroy is one of the best-preserved ghost towns in Central Ontario. Unsurprisingly, it has more than its share of ghostly inhabitants. Time seems to stand still in Ballycroy, and as long as it does the spirits will likely remain.

City of Collingwood Ghost Ship

Her hull is blackened by fire, and the rotting, bare ribs protrude from the sediment at the bottom of the bay; the dim light filtering down from above reveals the ship's carcass. Fish swim slowly through the shadows, oblivious to the aura of death and decay that hangs over the wreck, feeding among the hull where mariners met their demise. The sunken steamship *City of Collingwood* has long rested beneath the waves, thrown into the dustbin of history, a shipwreck forgotten by the community for which it was named.

But according to legend, on dark nights when the moon is but a sliver in the sky, the vessel rises from the depths, seaweed clinging to her hull, spectral crew busying themselves upon her deck. The ship glows faintly against the inky backdrop of the night, and wisps of fog roil around her waterline. Although the *City of Collingwood* was sent to the bottom of Georgian Bay by a raging inferno more than a century earlier, she looks seaworthy and none the worse for wear, as if ready to embark on a cruise upon the storm-tossed waters of Lake Huron.

But the steamship is doomed never to sail again. She rides upon the waves for but a few fleeting moments before once again being enveloped by the water, sucked back to her eternal resting place in the depths of the bay. The *City of Collingwood* is one of the countless victims of this body of water, and among the most tragic of its spectral fleet of ghost ships.

When the *City of Collingwood* was launched by the North Shore Navigation Company in 1893, she became the envy of the Lake Huron trade. The latest in a line of successful ships, she was a state-of-the art steamship that seamlessly blended functionality with sumptuous comfort for her passengers. The *City of Collingwood* became the flagship of the North Shore Navigation Company and, as its newest and finest vessel, was sent to Chicago to represent the company at the World's Fair that year. She was skippered by the company's most experienced hand, Captain William Bassett, a mariner with nearly 40 years of experience upon the Great Lakes, all of it without mishap.

From the start, the steamship spent its summers plying the waters of lakes Huron, Superior and Michigan, transporting passengers and all manner of goods between ports of call as diverse as Owen Sound, Mackinac, Parry Sound, Sault Ste. Marie, Duluth and Port Arthur (now Thunder Bay). Winters were spent in dry-dock at Collingwood.

Lake Huron can be a cruel mistress. Even in the calm of summer a raging storm of white-caps and winds can blow up at a moment's notice, swallowing up ships or driving them onto any one of the countless rocks and shoals that lie hidden just below the water's surface. Hundreds of vessels have fallen prey to her dangers over the years. And yet, thanks to the expert guidance of Captain Bassett, the *City of Collingwood* led a charmed existence. Under his exemplary command, not once did she suffer the slightest accident.

Unfortunately, the ship's luck seemed to turn when Bassett retired around the turn of the century. Soon thereafter, the *City of Collingwood* became plagued by accidents.

One hapless captain proceeded to run the ship aground on a shoal, and then less than a year later sink her in 110 feet of water off Cove Island in Georgian Bay. Only with great difficulty was the wreck raised from what could have been a watery grave, and at great expense was she restored to working order. The captain was relieved of command and replaced with Captain Wright.

If the North Shore Navigation Company was hoping to change the luck of what was formerly the crown jewel of their line, they had made a peculiar choice in selecting the ship's new master. Wright was a veteran skipper, sure enough, but trouble seemed to follow him wherever he went. Most recently, he had commanded the ill-fated *Atlantic*, which during a voyage in November 1903 he both ran aground on a shoal and then lost in a fire. His record hardly bode well for the *City of Collingwood*'s future.

Trouble was not long in finding the ship. On May 6, 1905, she ran aground on Bigsby Island, along the North Channel of Lake Huron. Captain Wright managed to extract her, but there was some damage both to the ship's hull and to his own reputation. Worse was to befall her only a month later.

The night of June 20, 1905, saw the *City of Collingwood* moored in the community for which she was named. Most of the crew was ashore, except for six men who were asleep below deck. Around 2 AM a stray ember from the smokestack started a fire aboard the ship that began to creep fore and aft. Alerted by three shrill whistles from a ship moored nearby, Captain Wright raced from his home to the docks. Seeing the flames rapidly spreading, he boarded his ship to attempt to contain the fire. By that point, however, the fire was out of control and it was apparent the ship was beyond saving. Wright turned his attention from fighting the flames to rescuing his crew. Unfortunately, he could save only two, his first mate and the ship's wheelman.

Four men perished in the ship-turned-funeral pyre: James Meade, fireman; Lyman Finch, deckhand; A. McLelland, deckhand; and an unidentified crewman who had joined the ship at Sault Ste. Marie. They died horrible deaths, either eaten alive by fire or strangled by choking smoke. The ship's hull could not absorb their screams. The trapped sailors' tortured wails echoed so loudly that those gathered on the wharves to fight the fire could hear them clearly, even above the crackle of the flames and the din of horrified onlookers.

At first Captain Wright had stoically forced himself to listen to their cries, as if it would bring the doomed men some comfort. He thought it was his responsibility as skipper to do so. But though he was not a man faint of heart, after a few agonizingly long moments Captain Wright could no longer bear it, and he found himself weeping and clamping his hands over his ears to drown out the screams. The experience of that night in 1905 would haunt his dreams for the remainder of his years.

After the fire had burned for two hours, the badly burned corpses of the four dead were removed from the charred hold. They were so badly disfigured that it was all but impossible to distinguish between them. It was also immediately apparent that the *City of Collingwood* was a total loss, having been ravaged beyond saving by the inferno. She had been razed to the waterline and the flames had burned so hot that even the engines were unsalvageable. Captain A. McDougall of Buffalo, who was in port at the time, reported that the wreck was the worst he ever saw.

The blackened remains of the *City of Collingwood* were towed to the west side of the harbour and scuttled. A wreck scarred from fire and the deaths of four helpless victims, she slid slowly beneath the waters, groaning mournfully as the bay swallowed her and she disappeared from view. Presumably the *City of Collingwood* lies there still, her charred timbers hidden under metres of water. But does she lie peacefully?

It's believed that extreme circumstances lead sometimes to the formation of ghosts, and terrible collective ordeals can permanently wound a location, leaving it stained by sorrow and death. Tales of unquiet battlefields where hundreds of men were slain are commonplace. According to legend, that's what happened to the *City of Collingwood* and the waters of Georgian Bay after the four sailors were burned alive in the hellish fire and the ravaged ship was laid to rest. Even though a century has passed and her broken hull is now partially buried by accumulated silt, the *City of Collingwood* seems to disbelieve that her voyages have come to an end and, on dark nights, she rises from the murky depths to sail out onto Lake Huron once more. She's a ghost ship, crewed by four spirits; though the bodies of the deceased were removed and buried in a consecrated cemetery, the flames that killed them seemed to sear their very souls into the ship's hull. Their ghastly spirits are trapped aboard the *City of Collingwood*, the lifeless hulk a nightmarish prison.

On an inky evening, with a bank of fog hovering over the frigid waters, the shadow of a large vessel might suddenly loom ahead. Sliding closer, the ship is eerily silent. There is no drumming of engines, no lapping of water against metal hull, no sound of men working aboard. The ship is enveloped in a deathly silence. As the ship draws closer still, her rusting hull and charred timbers become apparent, making her appear weary and wounded. A yawning chasm in the side is evidence of a mortal injury; water flows easily through to debris cluttering a cavernous hold. Loose timbers and unidentifiable wreckage float eerily in the quiet darkness. Then, unexpectedly, screams rend the night, cutting the silence like razor-sharp claws—this is a typical encounter with the *City of Collingwood*. There are, of course, variations, as the following account attests to.

Anthony Frodsham and his wife, Colleen, own a 42-foot cruiser ideal for boating on the Great Lakes. Anthony is an articulate, sensible, detail-oriented man. He doesn't seem to be easily excitable or easily rattled; he's a man used to being in control, both of his emotions and of his surroundings. But that carefully cultivated control suddenly disappeared one evening a few years ago, and he's still struggling to overcome the lasting effects.

The summer of 2006 found Anthony and Colleen enjoying a vacation boating on Lake Huron. They explored the rugged North Shore first, later making their way down toward the more serene shores of southern Georgian Bay, stopping for a night or two at quaint port towns such as Midland and Penetanguishene. The Frodshams were heading for their next port of call, Collingwood, when the temperature began to plummet. Angry black clouds rolled in, winds came screaming across the lake and the waves became rough, though not yet dangerous. Anthony knew a heavy storm was sweeping in, so he pushed his boat toward the safety of Collingwood's protective harbour.

The town had just come into view when rain began to fall in thick curtains. Without warning, a wall of darkness appeared off the port side. Anthony pulled back on the throttle and swung wide to avoid the shape, which by now he realized was a ship, and a big one at that. The startled boater called down to his wife in the galley, urging her to look out the window. Both of them noted how the ship looked dead in the water and drifting. The name *City of Collingwood* stood out clearly on a battered hull.

Sliding silently through the water, the derelict ship passed and began to disappear into the driving rain. Eyes wide, the couple watched for long minutes as the vessel grew small in the distance. They noted how not a single light glowed from her portholes, how an aura of age and decay clung to a hull clearly scarred by fire, and how there was no sign of life aboard. They instinctively knew it was a ghost ship and watched, transfixed, until it disappeared. Finally shaking off the paralyzing effect of the experience, Anthony turned the helm toward shore once more and sped toward the docks.

They were in their hotel room just as the sun began to set. Anthony crawled into bed to watch television, hoping to distract his mind from focusing on the earlier experience.

Colleen was more troubled by what they had seen. She took a long shower, trying to wash the clinging feel of terror from her skin. She stood under the pounding spray, letting the hot water work at the knotted muscles of her shoulders and back. After towelling off, she slipped between the sheets of the bed and, hugging her husband for comfort, fell asleep. Her dreams were filled with images of a dark ship crewed by tottering skeletons that leered angrily at her, chasing her through a dungeon-like hold filled with choking smoke and hellfire. The nightmare ended only when her tortured screams cut through the night and her worried husband gently nudged her awake.

The morning sun was still low on the horizon when the couple crawled from bed, sleep having eluded them since Colleen's nightmare had woken them. The first thing they did, before even heading for coffee, was to turn on their laptop and begin a web search for the *City of Collingwood* and what they knew must have been a terrible story. When at last they read of the devastating fire that had gutted the ship and claimed four lives, lumps formed in their throats. The horror of it all—the tragedy of a century earlier and their own unsettling experience—weighed heavily on them both. Even today, years later, it's hard for them to put into words the varied emotions they felt at the time and which continue to linger, at least in the dark recesses of their minds, to this day. It was certainly not something either one had expected to experience when they set out aboard their cruiser for a leisurely summer vacation.

Collingwood is a beautiful town teeming with energy, vigour and spectacular views of Lake Huron. It's worth a visit. But if you're venturing out onto the water, be aware that you run the risk of encountering a vessel far less full of life than the community for which it was named. Sightings of the *City of Collingwood* are blessedly rare, but everyone who has had the misfortune of sighting her hulk would rather she had remained resting in her watery grave. It's been more than a century, and still she rises to bedevil boaters. Who knows how long the ship will continue to haunt Lake Huron.

The blaze in which the *City of Collingwood* ended her existence ensured the once fabled ship would find a place in the history books, if only as a footnote. She was thus spared the ignominy of being beached and left to rot, unwanted and ultimately forgotten, as was the fate of so many of her contemporaries. But at what cost was her legacy assured? The very flames that immortalized the *City of Collingwood* also took the lives of four men, ended the career of the once proud steamship and doomed her to an eternity of restlessness beneath—and occasionally upon—the waters of Georgian Bay.

The Village Inn

Along the main street of Thornton, Ontario, a beautifully nostalgic Victorian building stands out on the rural streetscape. Originally a stagecoach hotel in the 19th century, over the years the building has housed a variety of businesses and is today a fine dining restaurant with a name, the Village Inn, that pays homage to its early roots. Many people have come and gone throughout the years, enjoying its rustic charm and timeless hospitality. Most have left happy, either refreshed after a good night's sleep or pleasantly full from a delicious meal. But for one tormented soul, leaving is something she tries to do over and over again, each attempt ending in failure that only prolongs her suffering. This woman is known locally as the "lady of the stairs," a tragic figure who paces the second floor, plays mischievous pranks and gives guests and staff alike an unexpected jolt by appearing suddenly out of thin air.

The lady of the stairs has been a part of local lore for as long as anyone can remember. Her story dates back to the late 1800s, probably sometime in the 1890s, during the period when the Queen's Hotel (as the Village Inn was then known) was at its height as a roadside inn. The Queen's Hotel had been established some four decades earlier by John Stewart, an especially ambitious and enterprising Irish settler who thought a hotel would thrive in Thornton, catering to travellers along the Essa Road (modern-day Highway 27) between Cookstown and Barrie. Wouldn't travellers, throats parched by the dusty road and bodies aching from the jarring ride, relish a respite during their journey?

Convinced success would be his if only he had the courage to take the leap of faith, Stewart decided to build a handsome hotel with a shaded verandah, comfortable rooms and a mezzanine looking out upon a well-appointed bar room.

Stewart's gamble paid off. The Queen's profited as the thrice-weekly stage dropped off tired, hungry and thirsty customers on its doorstep. The hotel hosted many guests during those years, but among the masses, one pair, a young couple, stood out. She was beautiful and gentle, her husband abusive and unfeeling. Their brief stay led to the haunting that chills the otherwise warm and inviting Village Inn to this day.

The story goes that on that night, the woman and her husband began to quarrel, and as it often did, the fight soon turned violent. The woman fell under a rain of insults and blows that left her body and spirit bruised. Suddenly, as if one of the blows had knocked some sense into her rattled brain, the woman decided enough was enough. She had endured the pain and humiliation too often over the years, but no more. This evening would be the last time her husband would ever turn her fair skin to an ugly purple. Overcome with an unfamiliar resolve, the woman fled from the guest room, determined to leave all her suffering behind.

Without turning to look back—there was nothing there but painful memories anyway—the woman raced across the mezzanine to the staircase. Fear coursed through her body, adding urgency to her steps. What if her husband followed and dragged her back? *I'll never go back*, she said to herself. *This time I'll be rid of him for good.*

Tragedy stains the otherwise cheerful Village Inn.

She began to race down the stairs, her feet skipping down worn steps, each one taken bringing her that much closer to freedom. Her determination turned to horror as her foot caught in her long gown. She teetered for a second, her arms flailing in an attempt to regain her balance, but the pull of gravity could not be broken and she fell. By the time she had come to rest at the bottom of the staircase, her body was broken and lifeless. In the end, the only way she could escape her abusive relationship was through death. Her husband had taken everything from her: her dignity, her self-worth, and in the end her life. But at last she was free.

Or was she? Those who have seen her tragic ghost and witnessed her antics believe that she is still trying to leave the building, that perhaps her soul is trapped there by the psychic echoes of her painful end. The lady of the stairs haunts the second floor of the restaurant. She can be seen standing atop the staircase, walking along the second floor mezzanine and looking mournfully down upon the village below from the second floor balcony. She appears most often on the anniversary of her death. According to former restaurant manager Dennis Naraj, a level-headed businessman, this is all much more than colourful legend. During his time at the Village Inn he witnessed several unexplainable events. One incident stands out.

It was shortly before the restaurant's 4:30 PM opening time. Dennis was in the building preparing for dinner service with only the chef for company. The two were chatting when they distinctly heard footsteps walking across the floor above them. The ominous footsteps were so pronounced that both men were sure someone was prowling around the second floor. Dennis and the chef immediately took to the staircase to confront the intruder, but a careful search of the building revealed that they were in fact alone. They were glad they hadn't come face to face with an intruder, but the absence of explanation for the sounds they clearly heard left them unnerved. During that adrenaline-filled episode, Dennis became a believer in the ghost stories he had heard so often before at the Village Inn. He has also seen lights turn on and off by themselves, and decorative pieces have moved as if being manipulated by unseen hands.

There was a lull in activity until journalist Sharon Bamford began investigating the story for a series entitled "Haunted Simcoe County" that appeared in the *Barrie Advance* in October 2005. Her enquiries apparently stirred up activity again, much to Dennis' frustration.

"Things were relatively quiet for a while, but after Sharon came by to research her story, the ghost began to act up. For no reason, two kegs froze solid in the fridge, which shouldn't happen…it had never happened before," said Dennis. "It happened twice in succession, but then not since. It was like Sharon asking questions disturbed the ghost's rest. Around the same time, psychics were upstairs and became very upset by the sensation of a presence. One of them was overcome by a wheezy feeling and had to leave in a hurry. It was a pretty powerful experience."

The Village Inn has a well-deserved reputation as an ideal setting for a romantic dinner. After all, the food is exquisite, the hospitality is gracious and the building is both intimate and rich in atmosphere. Recent renovations have turned back the clock to the glory days of the Queen's Hotel so that today it is a luxurious, welcoming homage to the Victorian era where polished wood railings, antique décor and soft illumination reminiscent of candlelight greet guests upon entering. And yet, at least two couples have found their candlelit dinners intruded upon by a spectral third party. Both couples were dining on the mezzanine, where the lady of the stairs began her ill-fated bid for freedom.

The first incident occurred years ago, at a time when part of the second floor was blocked off by a window-paned door that opened onto the mezzanine. Beyond were the former hotel's guest rooms, then being occupied as a private residence. The couple found the service, the ambience and the food absolutely delightful. It was in all respects a perfect evening—except for the strange lady who kept peering at them through the glass doors from the apartment beyond.

The lady of the stairs continues her bid for freedom to this day.

"The woman was distinct and appeared tangible and very real. When we first saw her looking at us through the door, we didn't think too much of it. It's only when it persisted that we started to think it rude and a little creepy," remembers Andree Naud, a level-headed interior decorator whose creativity lies in beautifying homes, not weaving fanciful tales. "Finally, I thought enough was enough, and I made a complaint about the leering woman. The colour literally drained from the waitress' face...there were no other women staff members on duty that night, nor was there a woman residing in the living quarters. In fact, those rooms were locked and inaccessible, so no one could possibly be in there. The woman staring out from behind the door all night, therefore, could only have been a ghost. It was my turn to have the colour drain from my face."

It was in October 2005 that our second couple visited the Village Inn. The day had awoken with glorious autumn sunlight, but during the couple's drive to Thornton, the weather had taken a turn for the worse and a light rain had started to fall. The sky was a gloomy charcoal colour, but it was not grey enough to darken the lovers' mood. They parked the car behind the restaurant and ran for the front entrance. During the dash the woman, Teri, happened to look up at the balcony above the doorway and saw standing there a forlorn woman looking out upon the village. She wore only a thin dress but seemed unmoved by the foul weather. For a brief second their eyes met and Teri felt an oppressive chill quiver her body. The woman looked so sad, so tragic. Teri felt her spirits suddenly become as grim as the sky above.

All throughout dinner, Teri struggled to enjoy herself. Nothing her husband said could lift the darkness that enveloped her, nor could she shake the cold that clung to her like a wet blanket. Finally, she excused herself and headed down to the bathroom. As she began descending the stairs, Teri was sure someone was following her. A floorboard behind her groaned under someone's weight. She spun around, but no one was there. In fact, there was no one on the mezzanine except for her husband, still seated patiently at the table. She took another step. *Creak*. There it was again, the distinct sound of someone following her, stalking her. Teri could almost feel a presence behind her on the stairs. Unnerved, she hurried onward.

A few moments later, Teri was standing at the bathroom sink and looking into the mirror. Her face was pale and ashen, her eyes haunted by sadness. Just what was bothering her? She couldn't explain why she was feeling so despondent and lonely during what should have been an intimate and pleasurable evening. Suddenly, Teri heard heeled footsteps approaching from behind. It sounded like another woman was in the bathroom with her, but she looked in the mirror and was very much alone. Still, the footsteps continued to approach, slowly and purposefully. The closer the footsteps came, the stronger Teri could feel the ghost's presence. It was a coldness that didn't merely chill the skin but also froze the soul. The footsteps stopped directly behind her. Her heart pounded in anticipation of what would happen next. She closed her eyes, whether to clear her vision or simply to await the inevitable, she cannot be certain. Suddenly, a bar of soap slid into the sink. That was all it took. The sound of the soap rattling around the drain broke Teri from her terror-inspired daze. She ran. And, understandably enough, the romantic dinner ended abruptly after that.

More recently, a woman named Tess had an even more unsettling experience at the Village Inn. For her, connecting with the despondent spirit brought back painful memories she had tried hard to bury and forget.

"It was a beautiful summer day when I went to the Village Inn for a quiet meal," she remembered. "My friend and I were seated in a dining area that was once the hotel's common room. Charm greeted us everywhere, from elegant old-fashioned furniture to splendid antiques that created an atmosphere of long ago. And yet, even before we were seated, an overwhelming feeling of sadness and anger took hold of me. I tried to enjoy myself and ignore the feelings that were consuming me, but as the day turned to evening it was harder and harder to do so. There was a sense of a connection to some unseen entity that hovered around us, a feeling of pain and sadness…the same pain and sadness that I myself felt many years ago."

Tess was married at a very young age to a man she believed was her prince, and for a time she was truly happy. But soon that all changed, and her husband became abusive. The pain she felt during those dark years in her life suddenly and quite unexpectedly came flooding back to her that evening at the Village Inn. She seemed to be tapping into the emotions of someone long dead and yet still tormented.

"Visions of a powerful hand striking a young woman as she cowered in the corner of the room took my breath away. I don't know if I saw it or sensed it, but it seemed so real to me. My past suddenly came back to me—the life I had for so many years, the life of living in constant fear. It seemed strange that such a beautiful and romantic place as the Village Inn would propel me back to such a tortured time in my life. But whereas I had definitely left that part of my life behind, I sensed that this spirit hadn't."

The vision suddenly faded as Tess' friend interrupted the silence by asking how her meal was. The two women finished their dinner, and afterward they decided to tour the remainder of the quaint old building and ventured up to the mezzanine on the second floor. There, where guest rooms were once located and where the lady of the stairs fell to her death, the sadness Tess felt earlier returned, stronger this time, tangible somehow. It was so unnerving that she was forced to flee the upper floor and cut her tour short. It was only much later, after reading Sharon Bamford's column in the *Barrie Advance*, that she learned of the local legend of the lady of the stairs, and her experience began to make sense.

Neither distance nor the passage of time have allowed Tess to completely escape the spirit, however. The experience at the Village Inn is still very much with her today, years later. She doesn't believe the ghost means any harm, but she does question what the lady of the stairs wants, and why she remains tied to the building after so many years have passed.

Perhaps the tragic figure longs for the loving relationship she lacked in life but sees among those dining at the restaurant. Perhaps she watches in envy couples enjoying each other's company. Or maybe she's still trying to escape from her abusive husband, doomed to relive her tragic flight until she at last gains her freedom. What if she wants help in escaping from her eternal prison, but simply can't ask? In any event, the woman's ghost will likely be permanently checked into the Village Inn, the final guest of a building that no longer serves as a hotel.

Aurora Heights Public School

Thousands of youngsters have passed happily through the halls of Aurora Heights Public School, a facility known for its academic standards and for fostering a nurturing environment for developing children. And yet for one child, the school is apparently a place of sorrow and restlessness, a tragic trap from which there is no escape.

Aurora is a thriving community located just north of Toronto. Having experienced explosive growth after World War II, much of the town—including Aurora Heights Public School—is modern and fresh. This town is not the sort of place one usually associates with spectral activity.

Appearances aside, however, Aurora is in fact one of the oldest communities in the province, having been settled in the earliest years of the 19th century. Urban legend suggests that Aurora Heights Public School was built over an old graveyard dating back to the initial settlement period, and many people have come to believe that a shadow from that era haunts the school's halls. The ghost in residence is said to be a young child, probably a girl. Some reports will have you believe there are actually two spectral youngsters eternally enrolled at the school.

Students and teachers alike have reported doors that open and shut, sometimes violently, of their own accord. There is never anyone around who could be responsible. This continues even though all the doors in the school have been replaced to stop the creepy phenomenon from frightening the children. Beyond doors that mysteriously open and close by themselves, the distinct sound of a ball bouncing down the halls is also heard on occasion. Many people believe this phantom ball is a sign of the ghostly girl's presence. Perhaps she's looking for a playmate, someone with whom she can play her games.

"I was alone in my room one morning preparing my lessons for the day when I heard a really hard slamming of the classroom door. It was so loud and forceful I just about jumped out of my chair," relates one former teacher via email, who asked that her name be withheld. "I was startled and went to go check the hall, but there was no one there. Then I heard a noise like someone was rustling the stuff around on my desk. Again, when I looked no one was there. It was eerie, and a little scary."

Another time, on a beautiful winter's day, a student turned his gaze to the yard, desperately wishing he were playing outside in the freshly fallen snow. He was daydreaming of building a snowman, throwing himself into the snow to make an angel or engaging his friends in a rousing snowball fight. His mind was snapped back to reality when he saw a ghostly handprint suddenly appear on the frosted pane in front of him. There was no obvious culprit; it just emerged from nowhere, the print of an invisible child's hand pressing up against the window.

Other accounts claim the voice of a young girl can be heard, or even mischievous giggling. She has also been seen skipping through the halls, all freckles and curls, dressed in an old-fashioned plaid dress.

Who is this child who haunts Aurora Heights? Did she attend the school and meet some unfortunate fate there, or is she perhaps a resident of the old graveyard who became upset at having her rest disturbed?

Among the young, imaginative students, an urban legend has spread that the girl died in a downstairs bathroom many years ago. There's no truth to this tale. However, an extensive search of the archives has turned up evidence to suggest that there may indeed have been a family cemetery, or at least several burials, upon the land now occupied by Aurora Heights Public School.

Lot 82 on the 1st Concession of King Township changed hands numerous times after the land was first granted for settlement in 1797. William Haines finally settled the property in 1803, and it remained in his family for 44 years. Mr. Haines had the misfortune of losing two children—both girls—before there were any established cemeteries in Aurora. It's likely, therefore, that both Rebecca, who died in 1804, and Polly, who died years later in 1818, were buried upon the family farm as was customary in those days. Is one or even both of these two children responsible for the hauntings at Aurora Heights? Their gender fits the tales. Certainly the fact that they died and were buried on the property is an eerie coincidence, at the very least.

There's another possibility. In 1847, the Andrews family purchased the Haines farm and remained there until 1902. They were Methodists, so when members of the clan died they were likely buried in the graveyard adjacent to Aurora's Methodist church. Unfortunately, they did not rest in peace. Some time ago, despite protests, many of the bodies in the burial ground were disinterred and moved to the much larger Aurora cemetery. The Methodist cemetery and those resting within it were further disturbed when the church itself was expanded and more bodies moved or built over. Might a youthful member of the Andrews family, feeling unsettled by the disruptions to her rest, have returned to the old homestead in search of comfort in the afterlife? Parapsychologists believe this sort of thing is actually quite common, and it would explain the presence of a spectral child at Aurora Heights Public School.

Historical evidence aside, what allows the ghost stories surrounding Aurora Heights Public School to endure is the numerous eyewitness accounts of unexplained, even frightening happenings within the building. Victoria is a young girl who, until recently, attended Aurora Heights. She says that the legend of the undead girl was well known among the student body and was the stuff of tall tales intended to scare one another. Still, she had a weird encounter that convinced her that this was no mere supernatural fairy tale.

It was after class and most of the kids had bolted through the doors. Victoria and her friend had stayed late to work on a project. The school, normally so loud with the sounds of feet racing through the halls, children talking and laughing and PA announcements over the intercom, was unnaturally quiet. Suddenly the silence was pierced by the pitiful sound of a girl moaning. It sounded like something from beyond the grave, a deathly groan of eternal suffering and sadness. Victoria's eyes bulged. She looked at her friend and saw terror on her face as well. There was a second long moan that sent shivers down both girls' spines. Victoria and her friend held their breath.

Long minutes passed with no sound but that of their hearts pounding against their chests, threatening to hammer their way out. Then, *bang!* The door to the neighbouring classroom suddenly slammed shut. The girls looked at one another. Neither one spoke. Driven by terror, they grabbed their school bags and raced from the classroom, not slowing until they burst through the doors and out into the schoolyard. It was only there, in the light of the sun and removed from the building, that they felt safe.

But perhaps they shouldn't have felt so secure. It's possible the ghost isn't bound by the walls of the school but roams freely over the land that once was part of her father's farmstead. One man believes his former home, located less than a block from Aurora Heights Public School on a lot that was part of the original Haines/Andrews family farm, was haunted. He wonders whether the spirit playing pranks in his house might have been the same one that haunts the school.

"We purchased our home in 1965. It's a very ordinary, working class bungalow. It was badly in need of paint inside and out but otherwise in good condition, not the sort of decrepit place that one typically associates with ghosts," he says. "And yet, the neighbourhood children also thought it was haunted. I assumed at the time that it was because the old gentleman who had owned the home previous had died in the house, or maybe it was the huge weeping willow tree out front. I later learned the neighbourhood children were right; the house was haunted."

He went on to describe his experiences. "Our cat would frequently arch his back and hiss at the blank wall at the top of the entrance stairs. Then my children and I started hearing music in the middle of the night, faint but definitely there. There was also the sound of bottles being thrown and broken, and what sounded like furniture falling or being thrown over. When we checked, searching the entire home, we found nothing had been moved and no sign of anything broken," he remembered, still perplexed almost 50 years later. "In time the phenomenon became more physical. There were several times when the top of my son's bookcase would come down with a crash, always when no one was in the room. It made no sense because the bookcase was otherwise stable. Someone would have to pull it down; it shouldn't have fallen by itself."

In 1968, the family decided to sell and move out of their spiritually active home. The man was taken aback when one of the movers stopped suddenly just inside the door, staring with saucer-eyes up the stairs at the very spot where the cat would hiss and arch. "Do you know this house is haunted?" the mover asked. "The little girl is sad to see you go."

Any misgivings he had about moving were suddenly gone. Years later, after reading a story in the local newspaper about the hauntings at Aurora Heights Public School, he began to ponder the possibility that *his* ghostly girl was the same as the one at his children's former school.

It's this sliver of possibility, this slightest chance that the tall tales long told by students and faculty may indeed have a basis in historical fact, that allows the ghost stories surrounding Aurora Heights Public School to endure. Whoever the spectral girl is, for whatever reason she wanders the halls, one thing is certain: at Aurora Heights, the term "school spirit" takes on new meaning.

Devil's Pulpit

The Caledon Hills are beloved for their tranquility, the natural beauty of rich forests and cascading streams, and the timelessness of the rugged peaks and sheer gullies. Few people realize, however, that the very vistas we cherish today were once stained with blood and malice. And while the taint of past horrors has been washed away by the passage of years, it has left in its wake a picturesque rock formation and a colourful legend that serve as reminders of this dark period in Caledon's distant history.

A high wall of solid rock, several hundred feet high in places, forms the south bank of the Credit River in the Caledon Hills, northwest of Toronto. In one place, a pulpit-shaped formation of rock has split off from the mainland, forming a distinctive landmark. Known as Devil's Pulpit, this geological feature has a tragic and malicious history that's perfectly in keeping with the sinister implications of its name. Murder, lust, warfare, suicide, demons, restless spirits…Devil's Pulpit has seen it all. If you look too long, too closely, this terrible past bursts forth into the present, and the result can be horrifying.

The origins of Devil's Pulpit stretch back into the mists of time, well before Europeans came to colonize North America. The legend goes that in these ancient times, two native tribes lived in the Caledon area, their villages located in the shadow of Caledon Mountain. The tribes lived an uneasy co-existence, but rarely did the simmering animosity boil over into open warfare.

That changed one day when a tall, handsome man fell hopelessly in love with a lovely girl from the rival tribe, the daughter of a proud chief. As is usually the case with star-crossed lovers, the two fell for each other at first sight. From the moment they met the two were inseparable, but because they came from enemy tribes their affair had to remain a secret. Each morning they would slip away from their villages and not return again until the sun had set and shadows had begun to stretch through the forest. While lying in one another's arms, the youths dreamt of a life together. Finally, one day they decided to make their dream a reality. Hand in hand, the young lovers went before the girl's father to seek his blessing in marriage. The young man sought to gain favour by presenting the chief with gifts of gold unearthed from rich veins found beneath his village.

Passion had blinded the two to the naivety of their request; it was unheard of for the tribes to intermarry. The elderly chief was unimpressed by the gifts of gold or by the suitor who begged for his daughter's hand in marriage. He refused to give permission for his daughter to marry him, and what's more, the chief was insulted by the young man's audacity. "What makes you think you are worthy of my daughter when not even the highest born among your tribe is good enough for her?" he asked angrily. "How dare you enter my home and insult me with such a preposterous proposal! You will not marry my daughter, nor will you ever lay eyes upon her again!"

Now barely able to contain his rage, the chief ordered the man to be led out of the village immediately and forbidden ever to return. Next, he turned his steely gaze upon his daughter and warned her against ever seeing the exiled man again. To defy him was to risk his wrath, and he assured her that his wrath would be more terrible than anything she could ever imagine.

That would have been that, except for the single-minded determination of the young man to have his love as his wife. When night came, he snuck back into the village, slipping from shadow to shadow as stealthy as a fox. When he came to the chief's daughter, he clapped strong hands over the mouth of the sleeping woman. She sprung awake, but before she could resist she was wrapped in powerful arms and carried away into the depths of the darkness. It wasn't until they reached the man's village on the edge of the cliff overlooking the river that she was set down again and released. When she saw who it was who had abducted her, her fear melted away and was replaced by joy. She fell into his arms, crying tears of happiness.

The mood, meanwhile, was less joyful in the girl's village. When the old chief discovered that his daughter was missing, he called together the warriors of his tribe and declared war on the enemy. The entire village was enraged and wanted to wreak bloody vengeance upon their enemies. Blades were sharpened, bows strung and arrows crafted, and men sang war chants to inspire themselves to feats of bravery. Prepared for battle, the band of warriors headed for enemy territory. Later that day the two sides met in a bloody but indecisive clash.

The initial attempt at recovering the chief's daughter having failed, years of ceaseless conflict followed. The forests ran crimson with the blood of hundreds of slain men, and vultures flocked to the area by the thousands, drawn by the taste of slaughter. Atrocity piled atop atrocity until no act, no matter how brutal, gave the people pause.

Horrified at the devastation performed in her name, the young woman grew despondent. She refused to eat, cried until her eyes were swollen and red, and lost the vibrancy that had first captured her husband's heart. She had made up her mind to die. In time, she simply withered away. Her husband could not imagine life without her, and so shortly after laying her to rest he took his own life by throwing himself off the cliff alongside the village. His broken body was left where it lay, allowing vultures and vermin to pick his bones clean of skin and flesh.

But even after the deaths of the young couple at the centre of the conflict, the fighting continued unabated. The senselessness of it all angered the gods, and they decided to send the god of lightning to teach a harsh lesson to the warring tribes. A fierce storm descended upon the land. Day turned to night, thunder roiled through the heavens, and lightning lanced out upon the devastated landscape. A bolt struck the cliff above the river, splitting the rock so that the longhouse of the man who had set off the cycle of violence was cut off from the mainland.

When the mountain was split, it released a nameless monster that had been trapped beneath it by the gods millennia before. The ravenous fiend began to scour the landscape, killing all the animals in the woods and the fish in the rivers in an attempt to sate its burning appetite. Starvation and disease wiped out the two warring tribes. The villages were left to rot, and in time nothing of either tribe was left except for the ominous rock that served as a reminder of the futility of war.

When Europeans began to settle the area, they learned of the tragic story and noted how the rock looked like a giant pulpit. Sensing the aura of evil that hung over the rock, and after encountering the restless spirits that lurk within its shadow, these newcomers named the formation Devil's Pulpit and came to believe the devil himself held sermons there. These rituals, said to be attended by the evil underbelly of society, were blasphemous mockeries of Christian services and involved sacrifices and orgies of flesh and food. After they were over, worshippers were tasked with subverting and poisoning society in the devil's name, bringing despair to all.

In the 200 years since Europeans established roots in the area, some people have claimed to have heard and seen unusual phenomena in the area. Something—the restless spirits of natives long dead, a devouring fiend, or perhaps even the lord of hell himself—haunts the area around Devil's Pulpit. There are times when the rational world falls away and dancing ghost lights appear amongst the trees, haunting wails play upon the wind and spectral figures seep from the shadows.

One of the first recorded incidents of this nature occurred in the late 19th century, when Caledon was still relatively young and sparsely settled. The frightful events as reported by Silas Peacock have been passed down through five generations, and though the tale perhaps grew taller with each telling, there is no escaping the fact that the poor blacksmith experienced something truly horrifying.

Silas found himself travelling one winter day. The deep snow slowed his progress so that by late afternoon he was well short of his destination. The sky darkened and sleet began to fall. A sudden gust of wind whipped snow around the legs of his horse and the animal snorted nervously, sidestepping on the road before the rider clicked his tongue a few times, calming it. The horse snorted worriedly again, ears turning toward the woods flanking the road and eyes darting. Silas pulled up the collar of his greatcoat to ward off the cold that had suddenly grown bitter. He squinted his eyes against the sleet, trying to see what was causing his mount to become skittish. Before him, Silas could just make out the jagged outline of Devil's Pulpit, but there was nothing in the woods to which he could attribute his horse's unusual behaviour. He leaned forward in the saddle to stroke the horse's neck, reassuring it. The horse's heavy breath steamed in the air.

A snow drift caught Silas' attention, its façade carved into swirls and spirals by the wind. Suddenly, a skeletal arm thrust from the drift. Snow flew outward as a figure emerged, with a grinning skull of bleached bone and empty eye sockets aglow with pale, unholy light. A clattering skeleton come to life, it moved toward Silas. The horse reared in panic and Silas tumbled from the saddle, landing on his back in the snow. He sat up just in time to watch his panicked horse disappear down the road, its racing hooves sending powder billowing high into the air.

Now it was his turn to run as well. He scrambled to his feet, but before he could take a single step he felt strong hands gripping his shoulders. Silas let out a shocked scream as he was thrown into the snow once again. On the way down, his head hit a tree trunk and left him dazed, unable to properly focus. He began to crawl for the woods. The leering skull looming over him seemed to break into a broad, sinister smile. Hollow laughter cackled from a non-existent throat. Silas tried to scramble away from the horror, but skeletal fingers wrapped around his leg and wouldn't let him go. The desperate blacksmith scrambled wildly against the pull and drove his foot into the bony, cackling face.

He broke free! Springing to his feet, Silas dove into the woods, seeking escape amongst the dense pines. Driven by unrestrained fear, he raced away from the apparition, through drifts waist deep and branches that lashed at his face. He was overwhelmed by a grim sense of danger; he was certain that if he paused to catch his breath, or even slowed for just a moment, the horror would be upon him. And so he ran, pushing himself beyond exhaustion until his breath came from his throat in deep, sobbing gasps. Suddenly, just when he thought he could run no farther, he burst out of the woods, all sense of direction lost. To his relief, he saw before him in the distance the dim glow of a light in a farmhouse window and trudged toward it.

Banging on the door, he was welcomed into the home by an aged man with wild wisps of white hair. The old farmer sat Silas by the fire to warm himself, then asked the blacksmith how it was that he came to be lost on a cruel winter evening. Though somewhat reluctant to share his story for fear of ridicule, Silas nonetheless related the terrifying events in detail. The farmer studied

Silas with black, beady eyes, and then in a raspy voice recounted a horror tale of his own—that of the tragic origins of Devil's Pulpit and the dark shadow it casts upon the landscape. At the end of the story, he leaned forward and delivered a sly wink: "I reckon you met one of the Indians killed in that senseless war, maybe even the lovestruck man himself."

There are many modern witnesses as well, their experiences showing that the passage of time has done little to quiet the restless spirits tied to Devil's Pulpit.

Elisabeth, who has lived in Caledon since childhood, has experienced some paranormal activity that she attributes to the nearby Devil's Pulpit. Her first encounter occurred in 1990, a year after she moved into a historic brick home with her parents. "I remember that night like it was yesterday. While I was in bed, I heard strange noises coming from the guest bedroom down the hall. It sounded like someone singing, and the harder I listened the more clear it became. I remember thinking it was the most beautiful sound I'd ever heard. I wasn't scared. Actually, I felt exhilarated and drawn to the singing. I wanted to go see if there was anything there. I darted down the hall and peeked inside the room. There was a large antique mirror on the wall, and inside the mirror I could see small bluish balls of light floating around in the reflection. The singing stopped abruptly, as if the spirit knew she had an audience, and within seconds the glowing balls faded away."

That was Elisabeth's first encounter with the singing spirit, but it wouldn't be the last. Beautiful songs carried through the home several times over the next few years, and each time the voice was seemingly more enchanting than before. She even had occasion to see the mysterious singer twice, though only for fleeting moments in each case.

"I was sitting at my desk doing homework when out of the corner of my eye I noticed a dark-haired woman in the hall. I turned to look at her, wondering who was in my house, but by the time I turned no one was there," she explains. "Another time when I heard the singing, I caught a quick glimpse of a slender, dark-haired and extremely beautiful Indian woman swaying gently to the notes. She vanished just as quickly as she had the first time I saw her."

There are numerous examples of paranormal activity around Devil's Pulpit, almost as though the rock formation is indeed an altar to evil. Ghostly fires burning atop the cliffs, the haunting sounds of spectral battle, pets that hiss and growl into the dark...such phenomena are reputed to be common in the area.

Some people believe the legend of Devil's Pulpit was fabricated by native people to scare off superstitious settlers and thereby keep for themselves the bountiful land and the rich veins of gold said to lie beneath it. Others, specifically those who have witnessed unspeakable horrors in the area, know that Devil's Pulpit is most certainly tainted by evil. You decide for yourself whether you believe the evil surrounding Devil's Pulpit is real or imagined, whether it really does radiate negative energy or is simply a landmark wrapped with colourful lore. You decide for yourself whether you want to brave supernatural terrors to determine the truth.

Ghosts of Discovery Harbour

Discovery Harbour, located in the town of Penetanguishene, is a recreated Royal Navy base that protected the Upper Great Lakes from American aggression for more than three decades in the early 19th century. Costumed guides, a dozen restored buildings and two period tall ships bring military history to life. But not everything one encounters here is recreated for modern tourists; the past literally lives on at Discovery Harbour in the form several restless spirits who maintain a tireless vigil over the base and represent authentic relics of an era long past.

The War of 1812 is 200 years old, ancient history as far as Canada and the United States are concerned. Today, these former enemies are now the closest of allies and the conflict between them is all but forgotten, rarely even taught in classrooms any longer. And yet, while the cannons no longer thunder and the sound of musket fire has disappeared, the echoes of this conflict continue to ring in numerous locations across Ontario. Ghostly battalions still march and do battle on several battlefields in Niagara, for example, and several period forts are stained not only by bloodshed but also by spiritual energy. Discovery Harbour is just one of many sites where spectral soldiers await a discharge that may never come.

The base itself dates back to the height of the War of 1812. The Battle of Lake Erie in 1813, in which American Commodore Oliver Hazzard Perry's squadron humbled the might Royal Navy, drastically shifted the naval balance of power on the Great Lakes. The British realized they needed a new fleet on Lake Huron and a protected anchorage in which to build and base it. Various sites were looked at, but the natural harbour at Penetanguishene was ultimately selected, and work began in earnest during the winter of 1813.

The war ended in 1814 before the naval base was completed, yet construction continued; Britain vowed never again to fall prey to American hostility. By 1819, the post was fully operational. The next decade represented the base's heyday, at which time it was home to half a dozen naval vessels and more than 100 navy personnel. A small army garrison defended the facilities. From there, famed hydrographer Henry Bayfield mapped lakes Huron and Superior, creating maritime charts so accurate they remained in use until recent memory.

Discovery Harbour—and its ghosts—serves as a reminder of our military past.

It was not a pleasant place to be stationed, however. The site was isolated from civilization, save for the small adjacent village of Penetanguishene, which was generally off-limits to all but the officers in any case. There was little the common soldier or sailor could do about the boredom, intemperate climate, disease, strict discipline and depravations they faced. Some deserted, some committed suicide, but most just endured.

It was only when the base was closed in the early 1850s that the garrison was released from the prison-like conditions and sent to other postings. Those men lying in the cemetery weren't so lucky. They were left behind at a posting they despised, a posting so remote and primitive it killed dozens. It's no wonder then that Discovery Harbour should be home to several restless souls that linger years later. Among these are literal brothers-in-arms who remain devoted to one another in death as they were in life, a young soldier who clings to his duty almost two centuries after freezing to death at his post, and a civilian bureaucrat who refuses to abandon his one-time home.

A rare opportunity to experience Discovery Harbour after dark occurs every Halloween during the annual Haunted Harbour event. Although the evening is dedicated mostly to youthful ghosts and goblins, adults enjoy walking along a candlelit path through the historic property. If, as many paranormal experts believe, ghosts are more active at night, then Haunted Harbour offers a unique opportunity to perhaps come face-to-face with a spirit out of the past.

Private James Drury

The blistering wind blasted off the frozen surface of Georgian Bay, pounding Private James Drury like a mallet. The cold cut through his overcoat, through skin and flesh, to gnaw at his bones. The young soldier buried his face in his woollen collar and pressed up against the rock wall of the officers' quarters in a desperate attempt to find shelter from the wind. He momentarily considered returning to the warmth of the barracks, but quickly put such thoughts out of his mind. To abandon one's post was a grievous offence and was punishable by lashing. No, Private Drury thought to himself, he would stand guard until relieved.

No longer having feeling in his hands, his musket slipped from his grip and fell into a snowdrift. He didn't even notice. Shivering uncontrollably, he slipped to his knees, bundling his coat about him. Private Drury began to drift in and out of consciousness as his bodily functions slowly shut down, literally freezing within him. Peering into the darkness and gale winds, he searched desperately for his relief, for the soldier who would arrive to stand guard outside the building and allow him to find warmth beside a roaring fire. "Where are you?" he cried, though his final words left his frost-caked lips in barely a whisper. With his glistening eyes locked on the empty darkness, Private Drury's dead body lay frozen against the wall of the officers' quarters.

Nearly 200 years after his sad and untimely death, his spirit remains shackled to the building over which he was ordered to stand guard. Private James Drury is the best known and most frequently encountered ghost at Discovery Harbour. Since his death in 1839, Private Drury has never ventured far from the officers' quarters and has made his presence known to generations of staff and tourists alike. Most of the time he confines himself to moving or hiding objects and making strange noises that alert people to his presence. Occasionally, startled witnesses have seen him in and around the building, still standing sentry all these years later. And while this phantom is generally harmless and benign, there are moments when he suddenly becomes frighteningly wrathful.

Bill Brodeur, the marketing and information officer for Huronia Historical Parks, is passionate about history and creating a positive narrative for Discovery Harbour that will attract tourists. And yet, even he is willing to admit there is something a bit unsettling about the officers' quarters. "Sometimes you can feel another presence in here," he said during a 2005 tour of the site. "Mostly it's not threatening, but there are times when it feels like something's not quite right."

Bill explained that many years ago a coworker of his, the interpretive and education officer for Discovery Harbour, whom he described as "a level-headed guy, not someone prone to making things up," was alone in the building performing some mundane task. It was a hot summer evening, yet he suddenly felt a bone-gnawing chill in the room. An eerie feeling enveloped him, and then he suddenly felt a violent blow to the back of his head, followed by an angry voice saying, "Get out; you don't belong here."

Thinking that perhaps his mind was playing tricks on him, the man tried to dismiss his fears and go about his business. A few seconds later he again heard the disembodied voice, more insistent this time and laced with malice, repeating itself: "Get out! Get out!"

At this point, the man decided it would be in his best interest to heed the ghost's warning and leave the building. Walking briskly toward the parking lot, he built up enough courage to look back at the building. He was certain that he saw a male figure standing in the window, intently watching as if to be sure he left the grounds. The figure in the window quickly disappeared, but the emotional trauma did not. Needless to say, Bill's friend was severely shaken by the ordeal. "He never felt the same way about the officers' quarters again. Every time he entered there was always the reminder of that frightening experience," Bill explained.

Perhaps the spirit of Private Drury, still standing guard over the building, considered the man to be trespassing in a building reserved for officers. Or, maybe, there are moments when the young soldier is overcome by anger and resentment, which might be understandable in light of the cruel manner in which he died.

The tragedy of Private James Drury's death is well-recorded by history and unfolds on an otherwise celebratory day: New Year's Eve, 1839. It was a particularly cold winter night, the kind that the garrison dreaded. Even huddled in their barracks there was no escape from the bite of the howling wind. That evening found Private Drury shivering at his post outside the officers' quarters. The officers themselves were all in town celebrating, but for Drury there was little to be joyful about. He was cold, tired, thoroughly miserable and resentful of his superiors.

The ghost of Private James Drury still stands guard over the officers' quarters.

Figuring that with everybody celebrating there was little chance of getting caught, Private Drury disobeyed orders by entering the officers' quarters to find some temporary shelter from the biting cold. He further broke regulations by helping himself to a bottle of sherry. He found comfort in the drink. Its warmth chased away the chills and reminded him of all those winter days as a young boy when he would sit at his mother's feet beside the roaring fire in the hearth. A tear stained his cheek as he thought of home, so many miles away. He longed to see it again. Private Drury poured himself a second glass, and then another, and then yet another. Soon, the bottle was empty and the young soldier thoroughly drunk. Only then did he stagger back to his post outside the building.

Tragically, though his thoughts travelled home to England, Private Drury never would. It wasn't long before the young soldier collapsed under the lethal combination of alcohol poisoning and exposure. He was found the next morning, stiffly slumped against the door of the officers' quarters. Salvation had been just a turn of the doorknob away, and yet he was too drunk, too weak from the cold to save himself.

The base's commanding officer couldn't have known when assigning Private Drury to guard duty that night that it would be an eternal watch for the young soldier. Almost two centuries have passed, and yet he has never been relieved of that lonely post. He's still there today, standing a lonely vigil, making his presence known in a number of unusual ways.

Many people claim to hear loud footsteps in the building when no one is there. And there are always other strange, unaccountable noises in the officers' quarters that have no natural source. The second floor in particular has a notorious reputation for unexplained noises. One woman, a curatorial assistant, claimed that one day while working alone in the building she heard a creaking noise from the second floor. To her ears, the sound closely resembled that of a chair rocking back and forth.

Suspecting a prank was being played on her by one of the park's interpreters, the woman went upstairs. As she climbed the steps, she noted that the rocking sound stopped. When the woman reached the second floor, she was somewhat surprised to discover that there was no one upstairs, nor was there a rocking chair anywhere that could have been responsible for the creaking sound. *So if there's no one here and no rocking chair, what made those noises?* she wondered. The realization that there was no earthly explanation sent a cold shiver down her spine. Frightened now, she raced down the stairs and out the front entrance. While fumbling with shaking fingers to lock the door, her breath suddenly caught in her throat. There, faintly echoing down from above, was the mysterious sound again: *Creak. Creak. Creak.*

The spectral soldier seems to have a playful side because objects routinely move about the building with no logical explanation. The most frequently hidden items are wine glasses and whisky bottles. Curators believe he is attempting to prevent others from falling prey to the drink as he did. But these aren't the only things mysteriously moved; other items are commonly stolen as well. Mostly they are just minor objects that reappear again a few days later, no harm done. There are times, however, when the misplaced items are far more valuable, and their disappearance is seen by staff as anything but amusing.

During a bout of unseasonably mild weather in December 1989, the officers' quarters experienced some unusually high humidity, which resulted in the walls and furnishings literally dripping with moisture. To prevent damage to the artifacts from mould growth, the curatorial staff packed all the valuable objects into boxes and took them to the dry environment of the Visitor Centre for storage. One box, containing an authentic Indian war club, a flask and stirrup hitchers, became lost in the rush. It couldn't be found, and no one recalled having moved it to the Visitor Centre. The curatorial staff were understandably upset at such important artifacts being unaccounted for. A thorough search was conducted over the next three weeks on both floors of the officers' quarters, within the Visitor's Centre, and even, in desperation, within other buildings on site. Still, the increasingly upset staff could find no sign of the missing box and its valuable contents.

One afternoon, the frustrated curatorial assistant stood in the mess hall of the officers' quarters and in half jest, half anger called out, "Okay, ghost, where did you put the darned box?" Something compelled her to search the building one last time. She went from room to room on the first floor, but found nothing. She wasn't really surprised; the building had been thoroughly searched several times already. Then she opened the door to the second floor, turned on the light to climb the stairs, and was stunned to find the missing box sitting on the landing above. While relieved to have recovered the artifacts, she was nearly floored by their sudden reappearance. It was just not possible that the box had simply been overlooked during previous searches. "Several people other than myself had looked in the building and not seen it. It simply wasn't there before. The box was sitting on a spot that I would have had to trip over the thing walking up," she said afterward.

One afternoon in the autumn of 1988, two members of the curatorial staff were in the building wrapping textiles in acid-free paper in preparation for winter storage. The shutters in the mess hall were opened that day to allow the bright sunshine to stream into the room. Since it was a gorgeous, unseasonably warm day—perhaps the last of its kind before the autumn chill began to settle in—the women left the main door open so they could feel the breeze and hear the chorus of birdcalls and the sounds of motorboats upon the bay.

The two women were deep into their work when all of a sudden a dark cloud blocked the sun, darkening the room in shadow. At the same time all of the outdoor noises died out, mysteriously muffled. One curator felt an almost electrical presence in the air that caused the hair on her neck to stand on end. She instantly knew they weren't alone, that an unseen presence had joined them in the room. The other staff member felt the same unusual sensation but was also horrified to see a white, filmy cloud float from the pantry to the servant's hall. Wispy tentacles flailed about as it floated past her vision. This was no coil of smoke or wind-blown dust, of that she was certain. This was something supernatural.

Within a few heartbeats the dark cloud had passed, the room was once again filled with light and the cheerful sounds of a fine autumn day, and the unsettling atmosphere in the building had lifted. It was clear to both women that the spectral soul that had interrupted their work was gone.

Curators have also seen the undead soldier looking as real as you or I. He'll be spotted sitting on one of the officer's beds and then, as if he knows that he's been caught somewhere off-limits to a mere private, he'll simply vanish. Startled witnesses are left wondering if their eyes had just played a trick on them. But then they notice the bed. The mattress is left dented, proof that someone had in fact been there moments before.

Other times, after the park is closed at night, staff will see out of the corner of their eye what they take to be a tourist walking through the building. When they approach to see if the person is lost or unaware that the museum is closed, he disappears before their eyes.

Visitors to the site have similarly seen the spectral soldier. One account took place in late summer in the late 1990s. Weather can change quickly along the shores of Georgian Bay, and where there had been clear skies just seconds before there were now big, black, rolling clouds. The air rumbled with thunder and lightning flashed. It was eerie and moody—perfect for a ghostly encounter. When Private Drury made his appearance, he was standing at attention in the doorway of the officers' quarters. He looked so real that a vacationing family took him for a youthful re-enactor. Then, as if he had been relieved of duty, he began to march across the grounds. It was only as he began to fade into the growing darkness that the onlookers realized just what they had witnessed.

Another time, a young boy standing alone in front of the officers' quarters caught the attention of a park interpreter. The boy just stood there, glued to the spot, intently staring at something in the building's doorway. He seemed confused and perhaps a little frightened, so the interpreter approached to check up on him. When asked if he was all right, the child just nodded absently, almost as if in a trance. The boy's parents came over and asked their son if he wanted to go inside the building. He shook his head. The parents tried to coax him in, figuring he was just a little intimidated by the old building. But still he refused. Nothing could make him enter. The parents asked why he wouldn't go inside. "Because the man doesn't want us to," the young boy said as he pointed at the seemingly empty doorway.

Some people, like Bill Brodeur's friend, have even experienced an overwhelming sense of dread while within the aged officers' quarters. A paranormal investigator entered the building one day with video camera and tape recorder. He sensed something unusual immediately upon entering and panned his camera to a corner where he was certain he saw a shadow move. "I know you're there," he announced. "Can you give me a sign?" He held his breath.

"I don't have to," said a hollow voice from nowhere in particular. The air in the room suddenly chilled and the lens of the camera fogged with the cold. There was an unmistakable aura of malice now, and he saw, for a fleeting moment, an ethereal form with depthless black eyes staring at him from the down a corridor. The investigator knew he wasn't wanted and wasn't about to push his luck, so he quickly left the building and its deathless guardian.

An interesting observation is that while he tends to be mischievous with women, the spirit inhabiting the officers' quarters seems to reserve his anger for males. Is this a reflection of Private Drury's resentment toward the officers who callously ordered him to stand guard during a frightful storm and then compounded the cruelty by neglecting to arrange for another soldier to relieve him during the night? It's possible.

Private James Drury died suddenly, unexpectedly and tragically. Not even realizing he's dead and no longer belongs to this world, he goes about the routines of his final task, standing eternally vigilant over the officers' quarters. The only thing that can release him from his duty and tenuous hold on life is the order from his commanding officer to stand down. With that man long dead and mouldering in his grave, such an order can never be given. As a result, Private Drury is doomed to remain a part of the experience at Discovery Harbour forever.

The McGarraty Brothers

On a dark, lonely stretch of frontier road, a young soldier clings to the lifeless body of his younger brother, not wanting to let go. He looks down at the pale, unmoving form in his arms and ponders his own mortality. In the middle of nowhere, awaiting the help that was promised him, life suddenly seems fragile and fleeting. He couldn't have been more right. By night's end he has joined his brother in death, their bodies intertwined alongside the road. The brothers, who were inseparable and loyally devoted to one another in life, are now spending eternity together at Discovery Harbour.

John and Samuel McGarraty, aged 25 and 23, were privates in the British 79th Regiment of Foot. This regiment, one of the few regular army units in Ontario during the early 19th century, dispatched small detachments to garrison isolated posts throughout the province. The base at Penetanguishene was one such outpost, and the most despised.

June 1831 saw a column of the 79th Foot on the move from Toronto to Penetanguishene. Within the ranks of the unit were the McGarraty brothers, young soldiers far from home who sought comfort in one another's presence. The troops marched in perfect unison out of the village of Kempenfelt along the Penetanguishene Road (modern-day Highway 93), providing a spectacular display of military precision. But successive days of marching in searing heat and oppressive humidity, weighed down by more than 60 pounds of kit and wearing heavy woollen uniforms, took a toll on the soldiers. It didn't help that the Penetanguishene Road was, despite its importance to the military, little more than a coarse, stump-ridden path winding its way through endless miles of wilderness.

The detachment was about halfway through its trek when Samuel McGarraty became ill and found it increasingly difficult to remain in step with his fellows. History doesn't record the exact nature of his sickness; it might have been sun stroke, exhaustion, dehydration or the sudden onset of any number of illnesses left unchecked and untreated in those days. Whatever the cause, with each step taken he grew weaker and more feverish. Supported by elder brother John, he trudged onward over the uneven road, feet dragging in the dirt, head lolling on his shoulders, his breath coming ragged and shallow in his chest. But the exertion required to keep up with the column began to break Samuel's body and spirit. Finally, he could go no farther and fell in a heap on the side of the road.

The officer in command was a hard, pitiless man. He refused to hold up the company for the sake of a single soldier, and with barely a twinge to his conscience ordered the column to leave McGarraty where he lay and press on to Penetanguishene. John was aghast at the order. He begged the officer to reconsider, but there was no changing his mind. John was unwilling to leave his brother behind. As the older brother, he had always looked out for Samuel and promised his parents no harm would come to him. John asked permission to remain behind to watch over the ailing Samuel.

Although he sneered at such sentimentalism, the officer agreed. A party with a stretcher would be sent back for them, the officer promised, once he and the balance of his men reached the base at Penetanguishene. Unfortunately, even assuming the men marched briskly and without break, relief would not arrive until the next day. In the meantime, the McGarraty brothers would have to endure a night alone in the dark, untamed woods.

As the sun set, deep shadows stretched through the forest and it became increasingly difficult for the McGarraty brothers to keep their fears at bay. Born and raised in England, they were unaccustomed to the night noises of the Canadian wilderness. They imagined each one represented a lurking threat—a pack of predatory wolves, a hungry bear ready to rip them apart with tooth and claw, or even a lawless bandit waiting to ambush them and rob them of their possessions. It was a terrifying ordeal.

Sometime during the night, illness claimed Samuel. He uttered a goodbye to his brother through parched lips in barely a whisper. With his glistening eyes locked on the face of his beloved brother, Samuel's body wilted in John's arms. He slipped away quietly, in the middle of nowhere, a world away from the English village he called home.

John was now left alone with only his racing imagination for company. To his frightened mind, every rustling of the bushes was a horror ready to take his life. He froze, trying to stifle the sound of his jagged breath so that he could listen for approaching dangers. Every second was counted by beats of his racing heart. Morning couldn't come fast enough. Tragically, John would never see the rising dawn chase away the darkness that enveloped him.

As promised, a relief party was dispatched from Penetanguishene immediately after sunrise the next morning to collect the brothers. When they arrived, they found both John and Samuel McGarraty dead. Samuel had succumbed to illness, while John had seemingly been claimed by the terrors of the night, literally scared to death by the imagined horrors of the forest. They were found lying in each other's arms, their bodies a mass of mosquito welts. The soldiers of the relief party hung their heads in solemn prayer for their fallen comrades, then gently lifted them into a cart and covered them with blankets.

The bodies were carried to the post at Penetanguishene and buried in the small cemetery there. Visitors to Discovery Harbour today can find this little graveyard with its sombre headstones hidden behind trees and foliage. The tombstone marking the McGarraty graves is original and dates back to 1831. It reads: "Erected by their comrades to the memory of Privates John and Samuel McGarraty, two brothers, late of the 79th Regiment, who died on the march to this post, on the 2nd of June, 1831. John aged 25, Samuel aged 23. In the midst of life we are death."

This stone is a reminder of the hardships experienced by the soldiers and sailors posted at Penetanguishene in its early days. So too are the tragic spirits of the deceased soldiers, who claw forth from their graves to haunt the grounds of Discovery Harbour. Sightings of two brothers floating side-by-side, marching in perfect unison with muskets over their shoulders, have been reported for years. Often they look so real, so tangible, that eyewitnesses are startled when the soldiers disappear before their very eyes.

John and Samuel McGarraty memorably made their presence known during the first Battle of Georgian Bay military re-enactment, a festival reliving the War of 1812 on Lake Huron that, after a few years of being at Discovery Harbour, has since moved to Wasaga Beach. The inaugural event took place over a weekend in late July, 1991. Many of the volunteer re-enactors stayed overnight in tents that were erected on the parade square, among them a photographer whose husband was playing the part of a soldier.

The McGarraty brothers do not rest easily in their graves.

The pre-dawn hours of Saturday morning found the woman tossing and turning in her cot. The humidity, even with the sun below the horizon, was oppressive. Her clothes clung to her with sweat, and she kicked the thin blanket away. Sleep eluded her. Frustrated, and resigned to the fact that she wouldn't doze off again, the woman climbed out of the bed, pushed open the tent flap and stepped out into the parade square. The mist that morning was thick and the ground was covered in dew. She took a glance at her watch, noticing irritably that it wasn't yet 5:30.

Sighing deeply, she decided to use the washrooms set up near the officers' quarters. The sun had not yet risen, but there was enough light that she was able to see without use of a flashlight. Approaching the washrooms, the woman was startled by the sight of two British soldiers in full regalia: red jackets, white leggings, tall black boots, shakos atop their heads, packs on their backs and muskets slung over their shoulders. The soldiers were standing at the southeast corner of the officers' quarters and were deep in conversation. She could hear their voices but couldn't make out the words; they were haunting whispers carried on the breeze coming in off the bay. Neither soldier seemed to notice her.

The woman assumed that perhaps these soldiers were members of a re-enactment group expected to arrive very early that morning, so their presence didn't seem particularly unusual. Intending to say hello, she started walking in their direction. She had taken only a few steps when she suddenly realized that she could actually see through the soldiers. As she stood there, rooted to the spot, the apparitions finally took notice of her. They stopped their conversation and turned to look at her. Their eyes were lifeless voids. Although no words passed between them, the two soldiers turned as one and, side-by-side, began walking along the east wall of the building. The woman noticed that now their bodies, from the waist down, trailed away into vaporous nothingness and almost blended with the morning mist.

After watching the two soldier-spectres disappear around the northeast corner, the woman was finally free of the fear paralyzing her. Audaciously, she decided to follow. But when she rounded the corner the two soldiers were nowhere to be seen. There was no place where they could have hidden. It was as if they had simply seeped into the mist and disappeared.

Still, the woman thought perhaps there was a rational explanation for what she had experienced. Maybe they were re-enactors after all, and perhaps the transparency was merely imagined? For the rest of the weekend, she spent considerable time looking for anyone who looked like those men or wore uniforms that matched theirs, but her search was fruitless. Nor could she find anyone who admitted to having been at the officers' quarters that morning. It was a complete puzzle.

There are those who believe that the McGarraty brothers also haunt isolated stretches of the old Penetanguishene Road, now widened and paved over as Highway 93. Stories tell of spectral soldiers caught in the glare of a car's headlights, only to disappear seconds later. It's possible that the ghosts of John and Samuel are doomed to continue the journey in death that they did not complete in life. When at last they arrive at the post, they perhaps haunt it for a short spell, and then return again to the site of their tragic deaths (somewhere between Wyebridge and Waverly) to begin the process anew. It's a cycle unlikely ever to be broken.

In life the McGarraty brothers could not be separated, so it is fitting that they remain together even in death. The two young soldiers continue to haunt the grounds of the reconstructed military post where they were laid to rest. Ultimately, this is not a story of tragic death, but of brotherly love and dedication stronger than death.

James Keating

Lightning flashed in the western sky out over the black expanse of Georgian Bay, illuminating the windows of the modest two storey, wood frame home. The military re-enactor, one of dozens on site to recreate the War of 1812 experience, brushed away hair that rain had plastered against his forehead. He looked up at a second floor window, uncertain whether his eyes had deceived him. Moments before, the man thought he had seen someone walking past that window, but it was a fleeting glimpse and he wasn't certain. There shouldn't be anyone in the building, he knew, and he was concerned that perhaps someone was trespassing.

The re-enactor approached the historic building and tested the door. It was securely locked. But even over the pelting of the rain on the wood shingle roof he could clearly hear heavy footsteps walking across the floor within. Puzzled, he peered through a window into the gloomy interior. He could make out the dark shape of furnishings. The hearth was black and cold, the fireplace empty. There was a hush about the place that was unsettling and added to his growing unease. He saw no sign of life, yet he could still hear the footsteps, heavy and determined, growing louder, approaching the window through which he peered. The man swallowed hard. He tried to shake away his panic. Someone—something—unseen was coming toward him. No longer able to deny the impulse to run, the man leaped from the porch, raced through the driving rain and put the haunted Keating House behind him.

If one man were to be associated with Penetanguishene's Discovery Harbour, one man who it can be said left his mark there, it would be James Keating. Not only was he one of the base's highest-ranking officials, but he also served at this forlorn posting for longer than any other individual in its entire history. Staff members have identified Keating House as a hive of ghostly activity, leading some to believe that he loyally remains at his posting, unable or unwilling to abandon the military base he called home for two decades in the 19th century.

James Keating was born in Ireland in 1786, and as a young man during the Napoleonic Wars he enrolled in the British Army. In 1812 the United States of America declared war on Britain with the intent of capturing Canada, igniting a war that would last three years and cost the lives of thousands of people on either side. Keating, then serving as a sergeant in the Royal Artillery, was sent to North America, and it was in the wilds of Canada that he made a name for himself. The young soldier was present at several of the more notable battles, and his skillful handling of cannons, which were always in short supply for the defence of Canada, proved decisive in several important engagements, including the Battle of Chrysler's Farm on November 11, 1813, and most notably the siege of Fort Shelby at Prairie du Chien in 1814. As a reward for his battlefield contributions, Keating was promoted to captain.

After the war, Keating left the army and became adjutant (a civilian general manager) at Fort Michilimackinac on Drummond Island, located in the western reaches of Lake Huron. In 1828, the commission set up to peacefully settle all border disputes between Canada and the United States awarded Drummond Island to the latter. As a result, the British garrison there, Keating and his family included, was forced to relocate to the naval establishment at Penetanguishene.

Owing to his experience in the role, Keating was assigned the position of adjutant at Penetanguishene and served in this capacity for 20 years. It was his responsibility to coordinate all aspects of the overall operation of the garrison, from paying the soldiers and arranging for supplies to ensuring upkeep and maintenance of the facilities. His main importance, in the estimation of Bill Brodeur, the marketing and information officer for Huronia Historical Parks, was "the continuity he provided for the military establishment at Penetanguishene. While other senior officers came and went as detachments were rotated, Keating was always on hand to ensure the seamless flow of organization and authority."

Penetanguishene was a lonely, isolated place to raise a family, tens of miles from the nearest real town and surrounded by bored, rowdy and more-often-than-not drunken soldiers and sailors. But there were benefits. His fine home was supplied by the British government, and all his worldly needs—from food to clothing to household supplies—were culled from military stores, allowing him and his family a standard of living well above that of the average settler. Keating enjoyed considerable prestige and influence both at the base and in the adjacent community of Penetanguishene, and he grew to genuinely love it there along the picturesque shore of Georgian Bay. It became home, and he never entertained ideas of leaving.

James Keating died in 1849 while still serving as adjutant of a facility that by then was on the verge of obsolescence and was slowly withering away. It was only a few years after his death that the base was closed, and in time both Keating and the base he served were all but forgotten. Thankfully, in the late 20th century the naval establishment rose again in the form of Discovery Harbour, a living history museum, and with it emerged renewed interest in James Keating, the man who held the place together for so many years. Keating House was rebuilt, and an Ontario provincial plaque dedicated to James Keating was erected out front.

Ask anyone who has ever worked at Keating House and they have little doubt that ghosts exist. If you work in the building long enough, you'll eventually meet the man of the house—in one form or another. Sometimes it's a subtle meeting characterized by mysterious noises coming from an empty room or a door swinging shut on its hinges. Other times, however, introductions with James Keating are more startling.

One interpreter, after seeing a cradle rocking on its own in one of the second floor bedrooms, bolted down the stairs and into the yard. It took all of her courage to even enter the home again, but she couldn't bring herself to climb the stairs to the second floor. She never returned upstairs; there was nothing anyone could do to ease her fears.

The majority of ghostly activity in the building seems to take place on the second floor, where all the Keating children were born—and where James passed away. One day in July 1989 saw another historical interpreter working in Keating House's kitchen. The day was unseasonably cold, rainy and gloomy. Predictably there were very few visitors during the morning. Still, the woman was confident that people would trickle through over the course of the afternoon, and in anticipation of their arrival, she turned her attention to making cookies for the park visitors. The interpreter was in the midst of mixing batter with a wooden spoon when she heard footsteps walking across the floorboards above her.

Thinking that somehow there was a visitor upstairs, even though she had not seen anyone enter, she went to the bottom of the stairs and called out a greeting. Her voice echoed through an empty home. There was no reply, but the footsteps suddenly stopped. The woman shrugged her shoulders. "Probably an animal in the walls," she said to herself. It certainly wouldn't be unusual,

and it seemed a reasonable explanation. No longer concerned, the interpreter returned to the kitchen and resumed
her work mixing the batter.

She hadn't been at it more than a minute or so when
the footsteps began again. There was the *thud-thud-thud*
of heavy feet, but this time paired with another even more
ominous sound. It sounded to the interpreter as if someone upstairs was dragging a heavy object, such as a box or
chest or even—heaven forbid—a body across the wooden
floor. A shudder passed through the woman's body and
she found herself gripping the table edge for support.
That was no animal.

Long seconds passed. The drumming of her heart
pounded in her ears. And still someone above was
labouring to drag a heavy object across the floor. Finally,
the woman gathered up enough courage to go upstairs to
investigate. Each step she took was harder than the one
before, certain that each one was taking her that much
closer to some unimaginable horror. By the time she got
to the top, her breath was coming in ragged gasps.

But there was nothing there. She looked in both rooms
on the second floor but saw no one and nothing amiss. She
even checked under the beds to see if someone was hiding;
she found no one. Now that she realized she was alone
upstairs, she began looking for another explanation for the
noises she had heard, something to satisfy her rational
mind and prevent her from coming to the terrifying
conclusion that an undead being was in the room with her.
In her search for a reasonable explanation the interpreter
even went so far as to knock on the walls to see if she could

hear animals running around within them. Try as she might, she found nothing that could have made the noises she had so distinctly heard.

Now terrified, the woman bolted from Keating House and went to find comfort in the companionship of a coworker. After relating her experience and calming down sufficiently, the woman agreed to return to the building, but only if accompanied by her coworker. Together they explored every possible source of the noise in an exhaustive search that took over an hour. Despite their efforts, they could not find a likely explanation. In the end, the shaken interpreter was forced to accept the fact that she had had a ghostly encounter.

Perhaps she could find some comfort in the knowledge that she wasn't alone. Many staff and visitors have reported experiencing a range of paranormal activity in Keating House. For example, often the southeast upstairs window, which looks out from the girls' bedroom, will open and close on its own. It's not unheard of for an interpreter to close the window just before locking the door at the end of the day and return in the morning to find it wide open. And it's not as if the wind could somehow be responsible because there's a wooden bar on the inside of the window that must be turned aside for the window to swing open inward. Similarly, there are times during the day when the window, opened just hours before, will be found mysteriously closed.

One afternoon in 2000, shortly before the park closed for the day, a staff member passed by Keating House and saw a man with brown hair looking out of a second floor window. She decided she should let him know that he would have to leave in a few minute's time, so she entered the building and went up to the room, but the man wasn't there. The door to the other bedroom creaked open. Spinning on her heel, the woman briskly walked toward that room. It too was empty. The staffer then went throughout the house looking for the mysterious stranger. Whoever he was, he was gone. There was no way for someone to get past her unnoticed, so the woman knew the person she had seen could only have been a ghost.

If you find yourself at Discovery Harbour, enter and explore Keating House. Let curiosity be your guide as you step back into history to learn about the challenges of raising a young family at an isolated military outpost. Learn the importance of the man for whom the home was named, a figure who, beyond his military service, played a significant role in the early development of the town of Penetanguishene. But while enjoying your tour, keep your senses alert to the unusual. That floorboard groaning overhead might be the sound of another tourist walking through the home, or it might be a ghost coming to greet you.

James Keating, who dedicated much of his life to the operation of the naval establishment, has taken dedication to an entirely new level. He's still there today, wandering his home, overseeing the base and providing unsuspecting staff and guests with bone-chilling brushes with the supernatural.

Ghost at Kotsy's

Heading for the restroom, you descend the stairs into the restaurant's basement. The dining room above is warm and sunny, but as you descend you feel a cold and unsettling presence. Perhaps you even hear a pitiful moan or groan, a deathly sound that crawls down your spine like an insect. It feels as if you're no longer alone. All thoughts of using the restroom are chased away as you hastily retreat back up the stairs. You're a little embarrassed that your courage failed you, but you find comfort in the knowledge that you're not alone in your fear. Many people before you have had similar experiences.

Kotsy's Restaurant in Bradford, a restaurant recently demolished, routinely served up spirits—not spirits of the alcoholic kind, but rather those of an otherworldly nature. Here, in this warm and friendly establishment, a ghost returned from beyond the grave to walk—and dine—among the living. It was a mischievous but shy entity, always eager to throw items around and cause a bit of mayhem, yet reluctant to show itself. While they never had a face or a name to the ghost, waitresses who worked at Kotsy's came to know it well.

Kotsy's was closed in 2009, and the building was later torn down to make way for a widened bypass intended to relieve congestion on the roads of a rapidly growing town. Soon after the restaurant was gone, customers moved on to other dining establishments where they could enjoy a home-cooked breakfast and a steaming mug of coffee. As a result, it certainly won't be long before the Bradford

Kotsy's is forgotten, and that seems tragic, somehow. While it may be okay for the business to slide into obscurity, doesn't the resident ghost—the trapped soul of a once-living person, after all—deserve to be remembered in some way? And we're left to wonder, now that the wrecking ball has completed its work and the rubble removed, has the spirit been left homeless and lost in a world he no longer recognizes?

You never would have known it from a casual glance, but the unremarkable building that housed Kotsy's had something of a troubled, even tragic past. At one point, a fine dining restaurant called the Bullfrog was located on the main floor, and in the basement, accessed through a side door almost hidden from the street, was a bar aptly named Secrets. This tavern, dimly lit for ambience, was among the more popular drinking spots in town. People gathered there to socialize, to unwind after a hectic workday, to drown their problems in beer and booze and to let their hair down for some fun. It was a cheerful place where everyone seemed to know one another, and the few times that alcohol got the better of guests, the offence was quickly laughed off.

What was less easily laughed off, however, was the fact that a patron supposedly met an untimely end in the building. The exact circumstances surrounding his death have been forgotten, but all stories agree that he died in the bar. It's possible that the emotional residue of this event stained the building until its very end and was responsible for a long list of poltergeist activity reported by staff and the occasional customer. How else does one explain the series of mysterious events experienced by employees at the restaurant right up until its closing in 2009?

"Jess" is an attractive, friendly, well-adjusted young woman who seems sincere in her belief that she had a run-in with the ghost one evening, but prefers to remain anonymous. She shared her story with us while pouring our morning coffee several years back, and you could see in her eyes that she was being genuine and had, understandably, been a bit puzzled by her experience.

The story unfolds late one night after the restaurant had closed and all the customers had gone. The hum of numerous conversations was replaced by an eerie silence. The only people in the building were Jess and her manager. "I went downstairs to mop the washrooms, and after I was done I put a 'wet floor' sign in the doorway to the men's bathroom and came back upstairs," related Jess. "Later, my manager asked me why the sign was lying at the bottom of the stairs. I had no idea what she was talking about, but she was right—the sign was lying on its side right at the foot of the stairs. I can't explain it; even if it had fallen over somehow, it couldn't have slid there. If you've seen the bathroom you know it's about 10 feet from the stairs."

We went downstairs ourselves to investigate. Jess was right. The doorway to the men's bathroom is indeed a fair distance from the stairs, too far for the sign to have simply fallen and slid. Perhaps more importantly, the doorway is at a right angle to the stairs. The sign would literally have to fly around a 90-degree corner to end up where it did. Someone, or perhaps something, had clearly moved it.

While that was her most dramatic experience, Jess noted that there were countless uneasy sensations and unusual sounds that collectively built toward the conclusion that the restaurant, and in particular the basement, was haunted. "It's creepy downstairs sometimes. I don't usually feel anything during the day, just at night when it's quiet in here. You just get the feeling you're not really alone," she said. "But I don't think it's a bad ghost. I'm never really scared. I just think it's a mischievous ghost who likes to move things around and make his presence known."

The young waitress' best friend, Katherine, who also worked at Kotsy's, had eerie experiences of her own. They came with the job description, or so it would seem. "This is going to sound weird, but it seems that every time I close the restaurant there's puke in the men's washroom," she told us in a 2007 interview. "The first time it happened, I just thought it was a drunk guy, and I shrugged it off as no big deal, nothing unusual. But it kept happening, and after a while you start to think, what are the odds that every time I close, some drunk guy comes in and pukes in the washroom?" Katherine shrugged her shoulders. "I don't know if it's a ghost or not, but it just seems like a huge coincidence…too huge to be explained normally. It sounds weird, I know, but I can't explain it and I can't help but think of the story of the guy who died in the basement years ago."

How does one explain it? It's certainly intriguing that the events related by Jess and Katherine occurred in the men's bathroom, located downstairs where for many years a bar was located. Does the psychic residue of drunken revelry still linger there? Is the spirit of an inebriated patron responsible for the phenomena that left the young waitresses questioning their own sanity? It seems to fit.

But not all unusual happenings occurred in the basement. Both women witnessed a metal coffee filter pull itself out of a coffee machine and fly across the counter, hitting a cash register several feet away with such force that the impact left it dented. We saw the filter ourselves and noted the damage; for a dent of that size it would have had to have been thrown with considerable force and not simply dropped on the floor. "There was no one around the counter, nothing to cause the filter to fly across the room," both women assert.

After having experienced a series of inexplicable events, no one could rightfully blame the young women for believing that the restaurant was haunted. They were convinced until the end that a ghost regularly patronized the restaurant.

Is the ghost that haunted Kotsy's the hapless victim of a tragic accident, as folklore suggests, or is he perhaps the spirit of a long-dead patron who returns to his favourite bar for liquid refreshment even after death? He may even be someone from the distant past, perhaps a settler who farmed the land long before the building was ever built. We'll likely never know the truth. Still, some people, while enjoying a meal at Kotsy's, made a habit of pulling up an extra chair on the chance that they might be joined by an unexpected and otherworldly guest.

Niagara Falls Aviary: Bird Kingdom

Darkness has descended over Niagara Falls. The lights of the Niagara Falls Museum have been turned out for the evening, and while the tourists have long left that building of strange antiques and unusual specimens from around the world, it isn't entirely free of human presence. A lone janitor goes about his regular routine, anonymously ensuring the exhibit halls are presentable by the time eager visitors arrive the next morning. Broom in hand, he sweeps the floors clean as he has done every night for years, his mind a million miles away. The janitor stops mid-stroke and turns quickly as a slight shuffling noise catches his ear. He scans the exhibit behind him but sees nothing unusual. Shrugging, dismissing the sound as a trick of the cavernous halls, the man goes back to work.

Unseen, a dark, twisted figure steps out from the shadow of a deep recess to loom behind the oblivious janitor bent over his broom. Lightning flashes outside, momentarily casting the interior of the museum in a pale blue glow. The janitor suddenly stops, breath caught in his throat, hair on the back of his neck standing alert. The light fades just as quickly as it appeared, but in those precious seconds he had noticed a shadow stretching across the floor, a shadow not of his making. It was a shadow with arms reaching out toward him, fingers of blackness about to close around his neck. Slowly, his heart pumping so loudly it echoes in his ears, the man turns.

He screams at what he sees, but his cries are drowned out by the thunderous roar of the storm raging outside. Standing before him is a withered and desiccated corpse, its malicious features hidden behind centuries-old funerary wrappings. It moves slowly, shambling on bony legs, its arms outstretched and clawing for the janitor with undead fingers. The mummy groans with the weight of the ages. Terror takes hold of the janitor. He drops his broom and flees into the night, never to return. The ancient horror returns to the shadows, where it dreams of a mythic era in the past when the pyramids were young and pharaohs ruled the desert.

This story sounds like something out of an old black-and-white horror film from the golden age of cinema. But what would you say if we told you this event actually took place, and that it occurred in the very same building that today houses one of the area's newest and most popular attractions? Sounds too outrageous to be true? Perhaps. Nevertheless, some say it did take place, exactly as written, joining a long list of haunting tales associated with the heritage building that today is home to Bird Kingdom and the Niagara Falls Aviary.

Bird Kingdom is one of Niagara Falls' premier attractions, perhaps second only to the majestic falls themselves. It is the world's largest indoor aviary, home to a chorus-like menagerie of several thousand colourful tropical birds from around the world. Visitors wind their way through a recreated jungle landscape that is as beautiful as it is serene, observing and occasionally interacting with the birds that fly and roost where they will. It's not the kind of place one associates with ghosts and the horrific. But just as Bird Kingdom includes a Creatures of the Night display, complete with bats, snakes, cockroaches and other creepy-crawlies that send shivers down your spine, so too does the building have a darker spiritual side tied to its past.

The four storey, concrete building that today houses the aviary has a long and varied history. It was built in 1908 by the Spirella Corset Company as a factory, and at one time the corset company was among Niagara Falls' largest employers, with 250 men and women on its payroll. The factory operated for half a century, but increased mechanization and reduced demand for its wares meant that by 1958 the business was employing only 30 workers. The owners realized it was time to move to a smaller facility.

The building wasn't empty for long, however. Within a year it was purchased by the Niagara Falls Museum, founded more than a century earlier in 1827 by English entrepreneur and antiquarian Thomas Barnett. The Niagara Falls Museum was one of North America's largest and oldest private museums, but despite this distinction it had never enjoyed a permanent home. Instead, the impressive exhibits that wowed countless viewers had shuttled back and forth between sites in Niagara Falls and even across the river in the United States for a time. When he purchased the former Spirella factory, Jacob Sherman, who years earlier had taken over the museum from the Barnett family, held out hope that this home would be a permanent one. The impressive collection included over 700,000 artifacts, 2000 photographs, nine Egyptian mummies and as many as four ghosts.

The Sherman family operated the museum until 1999, when the maintenance of the artifacts and the building became too costly. The museum was closed, the contents sold off to private collectors and the building put up for sale. In 2003, the Niagara Falls Aviary opened with more than 300 tropical birds and quickly became one of the most impressive attractions in a town bursting at the seams with sites and sounds competing for tourist attention. But while the building's function may have changed, some things have remained the same. At night, when the city darkens and the tourists crawl back to their hotel rooms in exhaustion, ghosts slink out from their shadowy hiding places to stake claim to the aviary, exploring its halls and exhibits just as they've done for decades.

Undead spirits occasionally disrupt the tranquility of the Niagara Falls Aviary.

The first, most commonly experienced ghost is said to be that of a former caretaker of the Spirella factory who, so the story goes, was so attached to his job that he returns to it every night, decades after his death. He is a friendly gentleman in faded overalls and a wool cap and is most often seen on the upper levels, bent over a broom as he sweeps the older parts of the building. No doubt, the spectral caretaker is simply continuing a routine he performed nightly while employed at the factory, unwilling to entrust the cleanliness of his beloved building to flesh-and-blood custodians. This was a man who loved his job, lived for it, found meaning in making certain the building was spotlessly clean each new day. It must be hard to let go of something that defines your life; in some extreme cases, such as this one, even death isn't enough to pry a person away.

Sometimes the ghostly janitor is witnessed going about his eternal tasks. More frequently, however, he isn't seen but rather heard, his happy whistles echoing through the empty hallways. When real, mortal janitors go in search of the source of the whistling, they find no one. The halls are silent, the doors are secured and there is no sign of forced entry. There's no explanation, nothing that a person can use to rationalize the experience away. At this point, even staff members who are reluctant to believe in the existence of the supernatural are forced to admit something entirely unexplainable caused the whistling.

Most of the night staff has grown accustomed to the ghost and is unconcerned by him. Some even relish his presence. After all, he generously assists the aviary janitors by performing minor, helpful tasks such as returning brooms carelessly left about to their closets. A mop pail once rolled slowly but decisively down a corridor, as if pushed by unseen hands, leaving the witness wide-eyed and understandably unnerved.

It's possible that misidentification accounts for the second ghost believed to haunt the aviary, that of a night watchman who slowly patrols the upper floors. When similarities in the eyewitness accounts are considered, it's easy to conclude that the watchman and the far more frequently sighted caretaker are in fact one and the same spectre. Both are seen almost exclusively on the upper floors in the older part of the building; both are seen only at night; and both are said to be men who whistle cheerfully as they make their rounds.

There's no mistaking the next resident ghost, however. He comes from a distant and foreign culture, originating in the dark jungles of the island of Java in Indonesia. This wizened old figure, a short, emaciated ruin of a man, represents a way of life that has disappeared. He's a figure out of time, clinging to a shadowy existence more than a hundred years after age claimed his tired body. And yet, he shows no sign of leaving the mortal plane anytime soon.

How did this out-of-place character travel literally around the world to take up residence in Niagara Falls? The answer to this question lies in the aviary's most unique feature: an authentic 19th-century Java house, the traditional abode of the indigenous people native to the island. This wooden building is a marvel to behold. The intricate craftsmanship, performed with primitive tools, is absolutely astonishing and matches the natural splendour of even the most flamboyant bird that now shares its home. But as impressive as the building may be, there's a perceptible sadness about it as well. In the 1800s, Java's Dutch colonial masters began a campaign to destroy the traditional way of life, of which these structures were an important part. Many were destroyed outright, while others were dismantled and used to create an exotic ambience in hotels across Asia. The Java house in the aviary may be the only complete one in existence anywhere in the world today.

As far as we know this exotic ghost has only ever been seen once, by a visitor who was stunned to see him standing—or more properly hovering, since his legs faded away below the knees—motionless within the beautifully restored Java house, a look of despair etched on his wrinkled, weary face. Another tourist sensed his presence rather than saw him. Upon entering the Java house, Leah "felt a heavy sadness weighing down on me, which seemed really unusual because the building itself brings to mind happy vacations spent on tropical islands. I could feel the presence of a spirit watching me intently; he seemed so sad and alone. Soon, his emotions became so strong they began to dampen my bright mood." Leah notes that the melancholy aura that clung to her like a wet shirt lifted once she left the building behind.

"I felt that the man was full of sadness because no one really knows what he sacrificed to build this work of art. The man put his heart and soul into the building, and he literally worked his fingers down to the bone to complete it, to pursue his craft," Leah relates sadly. "The Java house became his life, so much so he can't part with it in death. I also feel he's upset at the lack of respect shown by visitors; they walk through it, drink at the bar inside, take photos against its decorative walls, but don't have any appreciation for its symbolism. I guess that would upset me too."

Leah's experience, combined with the previous one, suggests that the spectral Javanese man is confined to the four walls of the Java house and doesn't have free rein of the aviary. He has never been seen or felt away from the building he built and loved.

Who knows for sure why the withered old man remains bound to the Java house? Perhaps it's as Leah sensed, a deep and abiding attachment to the building that he crafted with his own hands. It's also possible that he is so despondent and heartbroken because he mourns the loss of his people's way of life. Or maybe it's even more tragic, that the dark-grained wood of its floor disguises crimson blood stains, the result of a futile attempt by a venerable elder to resist the dismantling of his people's heritage. Intentionally or otherwise, he serves as a reminder of a lost culture and the destructive tendencies of mankind.

There is one final ghost connected to the aviary, a spirit with a royal pedigree second to none. He was torn from his royal tomb, smuggled out of his homeland and put on display for curious eyes to gawk at. He is Rameses I, Pharaoh of Egypt and a god amongst men. Rameses I ruled Egypt for only two short years, probably from 1292 to 1290 BC. He died suddenly and mysteriously, perhaps the victim of disease, more likely murdered. Rameses' end came so suddenly that construction on his tomb had barely begun and he was hastily interred in an unfinished burial structure. Sometime in the early 1800s, grave robbers stumbled upon his long-lost tomb. They cracked open the sealed entrance and were greeted by a gust of foul, stale air. Sunlight flooded into the vault for the first time in 3000 years, revealing ancient artifacts and a perfectly preserved mummy. Crooked, broken-toothed smiles stretched across the grave robbers' weathered faces. They had stumbled upon a fortune.

The mummy of Rameses I was sold to Dr. James Douglas and brought to Canada around 1860. It later became a prized part of the Niagara Falls Museum collection. People marvelled at its gruesome appearance—face stretched in the grin of death, eye sockets mere voids of darkness, skin entirely blackened, hands folded across the chest with no sign of the objects once held in them. On the surface, everything appeared to be fine. The mummy was a star attraction, and thousands of people flocked to see the relic of a civilization that had long since been consumed by the sands of the Sahara.

But over a period of a few years, more and more unusual events began to plague the museum. Strange sounds were heard, and under the pale light of the moon, shadows seemed to take on a life of their own. By the late 1920s, people began to whisper that the mummy's curse, an affliction made famous by the tragedies that befell those involved with the excavation of King Tut's tomb, was also at work in the Niagara Falls Museum. Some stories claim that horrified staff even reported seeing the mummy, or its spirit, shambling among the displays on blackened, withered limbs. It wasn't merely the desiccated features of the mummy or the suddenness of its appearance that horrified people, but also the realization on some level that before them tread a being that had seen the other side of death, knew its secrets, and through force of will alone had managed to return to punish the living.

Whether there truly was a curse at work, or whether the mummy actually walked around at night didn't really matter. What mattered was that stories began to circulate that sinister forces were at work, and that they originated in response to the violation of Rameses I being removed from the land he once ruled and put on display like a common artifact. Imagine the anger that must have burned within his withered heart. He should have been enjoying an eternal rest within the confines of his royal tomb, but instead he was ripped from the slumber of death when his vault was broken into and his corpse removed. The mummy's riled spirit found itself out of time, a god-king of an empire long since reduced to dust. If it sought vengeance on the living, one could almost understand why.

The stories took on a life of their own, fuelled by the occasional individual who came forward with a fresh tale of supernatural terror within the Niagara Falls Museum. This continued for decades, well after the museum moved into the old Spirella factory, until finally the owners decided to restore dignity to the dead king by returning him to Egypt. The question one must ask is whether the angry soul of Rameses I went with his dry husk of a body, or whether it was left behind, somehow bound to the building. No ashen-faced person has come forward with a report of having had a terrifying face-to-face encounter with an ancient corpse bound in age-haunted wrappings, so it's probably safe to say the pharoah rests easy in some distant museum.

The Spirella factory moved out of the building long ago. The Niagara Falls Museum is no longer operating. Corsets gave way to exhibits of unusual artifacts and strange specimens, which in turn have given way to hundreds of colourful tropical birds that take flight in a recreated rain-forest setting. And yet the ghosts remain. It's not difficult to see why. Bird Kingdom is serene and peaceful, with the cheerful chorus of birds singing and the mesmerizing sound of water cascading over a 10-metre waterfall. In a place so beautiful and tranquil, why would any soul want to leave?

Horse Island and the *Alice Hackett*

Georgian Bay is a tempestuous body of water, a cruel mistress that has claimed hundreds of vessels over the past 300 years. At no time of year is she more unpredictable, more deadly than in late autumn, when winter storms can descend upon the lake in mere minutes and turn placid waters into a raging sea of fury. One of the countless ships to feel Georgian Bay's wrath was the *Alice Hackett*, and the spiritual after-effects of her terrifying ordeal can still be found today on a tiny Lake Huron island known as Horse Island. Ghosts of the victims of this shipwreck were washed ashore like flotsam and have found no rescue despite the passage of almost two centuries. They are doomed to remain on Horse Island forever, spectral castaways on a barren rock.

The story begins in 1828 when the British possession of Drummond Island, located at the meeting of Lakes Michigan and Huron, was awarded to the United States by a commission set up to officially delineate the border between Canada and America. The military garrison, as well as more than a hundred civilians, were to be removed by the end of the year and reestablished at what is today Penetanguishene.

Throughout summer and early autumn, people were shuttled by ship between Drummond Island and their new home. And yet, October found some residents still remaining. One final vessel, the *Alice Hackett*, was sent to remove these final inhabitants, along with their worldly possessions and their livestock. By this time, however, white-capped swells were making Lake Huron frightfully turbulent, and all aboard were apprehensive as the ship set sail.

October is a poor time to sail the notoriously temperamental Lake Huron. Storms can descend at a moment's notice, with freezing rain or snow reducing visibility to near zero, and high winds threatening to either capsize ships or drive them onto one of countless rocky islands. It was a mariner's nightmare, but the skipper of the *Alice Hackett* had no choice. He had to sail.

The little sailing ship pulled out into the white-capped waters, and almost immediately she began to roll dangerously. The passengers, cramped within, were ashen-faced. One of the passengers, a tavern keeper by the name of Alexander Fraser, had brought 13 barrels of whisky with him. He had a brilliant idea: why not calm everyone's frayed nerves with a shot or two of whisky? It might make the voyage more bearable, he reasoned. Almost everyone eagerly agreed, and soon the whisky was flowing.

The ship's skipper wisely resisted the alcohol, and so his mind was clear as the *Alice Hackett* approached Devil's Gap, a particularly dangerous narrows between Fitzwilliam Island and the Bruce Peninsula. Devil's Gap was a graveyard for ships; dozens of broken vessels lay on the lakebed below, having fallen prey to the hidden shoals and unpredictable currents. The skipper of the *Alice Hackett* had no intention of adding to Devil's Gap's gruesome tally. Rather than risk running through the narrows under such foul conditions, he decided to beach the vessel on the shore of Fitzwilliam Island, off the southern tip of Manitoulin Island, and there wait out the storm.

Some of the passengers and crew, no doubt desperate to reach their destination and see the voyage behind them, urged the captain to press onward. But he was steadfast in his decision. He was not about to gamble the lives of everyone aboard in a winner-take-all game of chance with Mother Nature. Once the *Alice Hackett* had been securely grounded, her crew did their best to move the passengers and cargo to Fitzwilliam's shores, away from the pounding waves and sheltered from the worst of the storm. The livestock, consisting of four horses, eight cows, a dozen sheep and several pigs, had to be left behind; there was simply no way to safely off-load them.

Leaving the animals behind was perhaps forgivable. But there was no justification, no reasonable excuse, for leaving behind a young mother and her 10-year-old daughter, Therese. It seems simply that the crew, and even her husband, had been so drunk that they had unwittingly left Angelique Lepine and her daughter behind, and that by the time they realized their mistake the storm had grown so furious that a rescue was all but impossible.

Aboard the *Alice Hackett*, Angelique huddled among the shifting cargo, white-knuckles holding her wailing daughter tightly to her chest. She was terrified. It sounded as if the ship would be ripped apart at any moment; waves lashed against the hull, the keel ground against rocks below, and the wood seemed to groan under the relentless assault.

Suddenly, a cannon broke loose of its moorings, crashed against the hull and pierced a hole in the ship's side. Icy water began pouring into the stricken ship, filling her holds. Angelique and Therese raced up to the deck to escape the rapidly rising waters, but there they found themselves buffeted by the gale-force winds. Fearing that they would be swept overboard, Angelique tied her daughter to her back with a length of rope and then tied herself to the mast.

Stung by the driving rain, her strength drained by the cold, she clung to the mast for dear life. Below her, waves hammered against the vessel and the animals cried out in terror. One by one, the livestock were swept out to sea and pulled under by the waves. Each time one disappeared beneath the frigid water, its eyes wide in terror, Angelique's heart tore open. Frightened that she would share a similar fate, Angelique searched the darkness for some sign of her husband or the crew, anyone who might rescue her and her child, but to no avail. She was truly alone, a prisoner aboard the battered ship until the howling wind and driving rain abated.

The storm eventually blew over. The water returned to an eerie calm, but the crew of the *Alice Hackett* returned to the vessel with heavy hearts. Surely Angelique and Therese could not have survived the savage storm, they all thought. Yet, when they climbed aboard, there they were, limp against the mast, unconscious and exhausted, but still very much alive. Although surely traumatized, both of them emerged from the ordeal physically unscathed.

A ghostly *Alice Hackett* is said to appear during stormy weather.

The *Alice Hackett*'s passengers became among the first to settle Penetanguishene, providing the community and its area with a Francophone character that can still occasionally be felt to this day. But one of the ship's passengers had been left behind, stranded on the windswept, barren island. A horse had managed to escape from the sinking *Alice Hackett* and swim through the raging surf to get to shore. Its owner was thrilled that it had survived, but then was heartbroken when the rescue ship arrived and proved too crowded to take the horse aboard. The owner tearfully hugged its neck and gently stroked its face. He hated leaving the horse to its fate on the desolate island, but solemnly promised not to forget him and to return for him as soon as possible.

Unfortunately, while the man intended to be true to his word, he wasn't able to find a captain willing to take him back to the island that late in the season. The danger was just too great; to risk a ship to rescue a horse seemed foolhardy. In the end, the owner never did go back. The horse lived out its natural existence alone on the barren rock, and for many years after, Fitzwilliam Island was known as Horse Island.

Eerily, there are countless tales to suggest that the horse—or at least its spirit—still resides upon the otherwise uninhabited isle, waiting for its owner to return and rescue it. For almost 200 years, mariners aboard passing ships have reported seeing a majestic white stallion, often glowing with luminescence, galloping along the rocky shore. Most often, this spectral stallion is seen on dark and blustery evenings in October, conditions which mirror those under which the *Alice Hackett* was beached and the horse marooned. If the stories are true, the horse's spirit is doomed to continue what must have been a lonely existence upon Fitzwilliam Island for all eternity, never knowing peace or companionship, hoping for a rescue that will never occur.

It's possible that the ghostly stallion is not entirely alone on Horse Island. There are reports that during stormy weather, the harrowing ordeal of the *Alice Hackett* is recreated—the terror of a near-disastrous night replayed. The ship is seen rolling on its side, water rushing into its hold through a terrible gash in its hull, its demise seemingly near at hand. Over the howl of the wind and the pelting of rain the screams of a terrified mother and daughter can be heard, cries so heavy with fear and anguish that they tear at the heart of even the hardiest of men. The phantom ship is so clear that, when it's first seen, the witness presumes it is an actual sailing vessel. It soon becomes evident, however, that the ship is an illusion; no vessel of that design has sailed the Great Lakes in many, many years. As awestruck mariners watch in silent terror, the image vanishes from view as mysteriously and quickly as it had appeared.

On occasion, the phantom vessel is heard but not seen. One crew aboard a steamship experienced this phenomenon as they were making their way to Collingwood. Weather had closed in. The fog surrounding their ship was as dense as anyone aboard could ever remember seeing. The ship's captain ordered that the speed be reduced. As the thrum of the engine subsided, the cries of a woman could be heard coming from out of the fogbank. This continued for several long minutes. The crew felt powerless, sure that somewhere nearby a woman was in distress, and they were unable to come to her rescue. When the fog suddenly lifted sometime later, the lake was eerily calm and eerily empty. There was no evidence of a vessel in trouble, no sign of wreckage to suggest a ship went down, and no more desperate cries for help. When it was later found out that no vessels had gone missing in that stretch of water, the crew was left with only one explanation: they had heard the phantom cries of Angelique Lepine echoing out over the decades.

It seems that even though Angelique and her daughter, Therese, survived the storm, the terror they experienced that night in 1828 has tainted the water in some way, so that instead of resting peacefully in their earthen graves, their spirits return to this God-forsaken isle. The trauma of that

October night pulls their spirits back to Horse Island, where in death they are condemned to relive the experience that haunted their dreams in life.

Lake Huron is a majestic and ruggedly beautiful body of water, but it can also be a sinister place where powerful storms overwhelm unsuspecting ships and claim the lives of passengers and crew. Those aboard the *Alice Hackett* knew all too well the terrible wrath of this Great Lake; they experienced it first-hand. They also came to realize, in the years that followed, that though they had moved on with their lives, that autumn night in 1828 was not so easily left in the past. The ghostly legends surrounding Horse Island helped keep the painful wounds fresh and unhealed: the glowing stallion left behind by its owner, loyal to the grave and beyond; a helpless mother and daughter, left to their fates aboard a wrecked ship by drunk and uncaring passengers, whose cries for help echo out from beyond the grave; and a vessel that is torn apart by a storm in an annual re-enactment of a terrifying event many years ago.

Perhaps one day the spectral horse will cross over to a heavenly pasture, Angelique and Therese will leave their nightmare behind and find peace in their graves, and the *Alice Hackett* will go to eternal dry dock. Only then will everyone involved—ship and passengers alike—complete a voyage begun almost 200 years ago. Only then will that October day in 1828 truly end.

Georgina Pioneer Village: Noble House

The sound of doors creaking on rusty hinges is plainly heard, and yet there are no doors to be found. From somewhere in the darkened building comes a faint sound of piteous crying. Footsteps creep across the floorboards of an empty hallway. A dark shadow passes before a window, and pale blue moonlight reveals the figure of a woman that suddenly disappears. Noble House is infamous for a range of haunted activity.

And yet none of this was on Melissa Matt's mind as she walked quickly through the 19th-century streets at Georgina Pioneer Village toward the historic building. Although her title is archives coordinator, her job description goes well beyond managing dusty texts and yellowed papers. On this day she and a colleague were tasked with cleaning Noble House, and since it is by far the largest building on site, it would take some time to complete the chore. The sooner they got started, the sooner they would be finished.

Together, the two women began cleaning the period home. They had no time to admire the beautiful furnishings and décor that brought the building to life as it had looked when it was the residence of the prosperous physician, Doctor Charles Noble. They barely had time to chat, working in separate rooms and rarely taking breaks. Upon completing the first floor, they made their way up to the second. Melissa began cleaning the child's room while the other woman set to work in the master bedroom.

Despite its benign appearance, Noble House is almost certainly haunted.

Several minutes later, Melissa looked up to see her colleague standing in the doorway. She was pale and looked shaken. "Were you just in the master bedroom?" she asked, a hint of agitation in her voice. Melissa truthfully responded that she was not; she hadn't left the child's room once. The other woman closely studied her face, clearly trying to determine if she was being lied to. Melissa had a well-deserved reputation as a prankster, once locking her coworker in the train station, which she was deathly afraid of due to stories of ghostly activity. However, today Melissa had been in no mood for games.

"Why do you ask?" Melissa finally said, breaking the awkward silence. Her coworker explained that as she was leaning over a dresser drawer she heard as clear as day a female whisper in her ear, but when she turned around she was alone in the room. She didn't really believe it had been Melissa—how would she have escaped unseen and unheard—but perhaps held out some sliver of hope that it had been so her she didn't have to struggle with the reality that a ghost had been watching unseen as she worked.

In truth, neither Melissa nor her coworker should have been surprised by the incident. After all, Noble House has a tradition of paranormal activity and haunting encounters that goes back years. Interestingly, and perhaps not coincidentally, the resident spirit seems to have become more active since restorations of Noble House began a few years ago. It's as if when the restorers lifted rotting floorboards and tore down crumbling plaster walls, they released a spirit long trapped.

Noble House is far from the iconic image of a haunted house. Yellowed and rotting drapes don't flutter like phantoms in broken windows, the front door doesn't swing open on rusted hinges, daring people to enter, and the floorboards don't groan ominously, like a corpse clawing its way up from a fresh grave, as you walk from room to room. Instead, Noble House is a beautifully restored, charming heritage home with bright rooms and an atmosphere of refinement and relaxed wealth. One wouldn't expect supernatural encounters to occur in such a place.

And yet, some people who enter report a shiver going down their spine and begin having the uncomfortable sensation that someone is hiding, lurking, watching them. When the home was moved from its original location in nearby Sutton to the grounds of Georgina Pioneer Village, someone must have come along with it, a prior inhabitant bound to the land of the living by a deep personal connection to the building and a story of terrible suffering that makes it impossible to rest.

A few years ago, a ghost-hunting team spent the night at Georgina Pioneer Village, conducting experiments both scientific and psychic to catalogue the spirits in the museum. The village's undead population was particularly active that night, providing ample evidence of their existence. When the bleary-eyed team left in the morning after an all-night vigil, they were convinced several buildings on site were haunted. The Mann House, long rumoured to have several restless entities in residence (including shy children and a woman in a long, dark gown), was the scene of exciting orb activity that was caught on camera. Across the road, an unusual glow, like that given off by a sputtering candle, was seen in the blacksmith shop. And in the general store, a psychic sensed the presence of an unseen gentleman with a long, dark beard and dressed in a suit of days gone by.

But of all the historic buildings carefully restored and preserved at Georgina Pioneer Village, the impressive Noble House is the most spiritually active. The ghost of a lonely and heartbroken woman, weary with grief after having been separated from her loved ones for what must seem like an eternity, bemoans her tragic fate within the home.

Over the years, several people, staff and visitors alike, have had encounters with this mournful spirit. One woman was shocked when an icy chill began caressing her face in one of the upstairs bedrooms. Her breath began to mist before her face, even though it was a stifling hot summer day and she had only moments before been sweating. This was followed by the sound of a child crying, a soft but heart-wrenching wail that broke her heart to listen to. She searched the building room by room, expecting to find a child separated from his family, but was surprised to find no one. She noted that when the crying stopped, the mysterious cold that clung to her seemed to melt away.

Denis has visited Georgina Pioneer Village several times over the years in his role as a historical re-enactor. A beard, bushy and dense, obscures much of the man's weathered face, making him look more like Grizzly Adams than a British soldier. But he wears the distinctive British red coat and over his shoulder hangs the brown-bess musket carried by Britain's soldiers into countless battles throughout the 19th century. His costume makes him look the part, and he takes pride in acting the part.

A long-time War of 1812-era re-enactor, this time he's at Georgina Pioneer Village to participate in March to Rebellion, a two-day event reliving William Lyon Mackenzie's ill-fated 1837 uprising in Ontario. It's the second year he's taken part in the living history festival, and there's nothing he likes better than discussing history or firing his musket in mock battle. This evening, however, he's not here to talk about soldiering. Instead, he chooses to talk about ghosts and the frightful experience he had on these very grounds during the previous year's rebellion re-enactment.

"It was around nine o'clock at night. We were sitting around the campfire, talking and relaxing after the day's events. Mostly I guess we were trying to stay warm, because it had rained most of the day and was unseasonably cool.

It was miserable. The grounds were a quagmire of mud and we were chilled to the bone. But there's nothing like a roaring fire to make you feel better," he said, thinking back.

"After an hour or so, people started to wander off to bed. As re-enactors we usually sleep in tents as period soldiers would have done, but it was so cold and wet we decided to roll our blankets out in the schoolhouse instead. I was just about to call it a night when I thought I saw a light on in the upper floor of Noble House. I thought maybe a candle or lantern hadn't been extinguished, so I grabbed a lantern and headed off to see. I probably shouldn't have."

Pushing open the door, he entered the historic home and headed directly for the second floor, his footsteps echoing loudly in the empty building as his boots thumped up the wooden stairs. He was halfway down the upstairs hallway, headed toward the front room from which he saw the flickering light, when his lantern suddenly blew out and he found himself cast into absolute blackness. It was as if a cloak had been thrown over the house. He squinted into the darkness, hoping to make out the shape of a door or window—anything. But the blackness that surrounded him was darker than the sky of a starless night.

Suddenly, a shimmering figure appeared not more than five feet in front of him. It was a woman dressed in a gown, and she seemed to glow like pale moonlight. He reached out to her, without knowing why. She seemed to flow away from his hands, as though tempting him to follow. He didn't dare. Instead, with icy fear gripping his heart, he felt for the wall and slowly, back pressed against the cool plaster, retraced his path toward the staircase and the exit below. He half-expected to see the unquiet spirit coming after him, angry at having been spurned. Terror formed a hard lump in his throat and drove him to greater speed. Finally, after what seemed like an eternity, his feet met stairs and he descended toward safety.

"I sat alone by the fire for a while afterward that night," he remembers, his voice barely a whisper. "I was shaking. I held my quivering hands, trying to settle them. I was a mess. I've never been so scared in my life, and you couldn't pay me enough to go back into that building after dark."

The spectral woman made an appearance at another special event as well. It was a cold yet pleasant night in December when Amanda and Richard decided to experience the museum's annual Old Tyme Christmas Festival. They wanted to see what the yuletide season would have been like in the 19th century. It was their first visit to the pioneer village, and they were soon swept up in the magic of the event. There were no fancy Christmas lights, just the simple glow of candles burning; no fancy decorations, just ones that had been made with love and care by someone's hands. With snow lightly falling from above, there was a serene and peaceful feeling to the evening.

Each of the museum's 14 carefully restored period buildings was decorated to reflect an authentic pioneer Christmas. Amanda and Richard enjoyed hot apple cider and gingerbread cookies in a shadowy, lamp-lit log cabin, watched the blacksmith work his trade in his smithy, warmed themselves by the pot-bellied stove in the Sutton West Train Station, and shopped for presents at the Vanderburgh General Store. Each building entered seemed more enchanting than the last. The tune of Victorian carols filtered out of the one-room schoolhouse, drifting lazily upon the crisp air. To the young friends, it really felt like they had been transported back in time.

But it was Noble House, the largest and most refined building on site, that proved most memorable. Immediately upon stepping inside, they could feel that there was something special and unique about this home. They couldn't help but linger in its warm confines. The home was beautifully decorated for the occasion, and the enchanting sounds of the harpsichord and windpipe added tranquility to the setting. This place gave the impression that at one time it was host to grand parties, and indeed the laughter of people huddled around the musicians could be heard throughout the home.

Here, more than anywhere else in the village, Amanda felt as if she had been transported into the 19th century and had been issued a personal invitation to a private party. It was simply heart-warming. But there was more to this place, and her connection with the past would become more intimate, more real, than Amanda could ever have imagined.

Sneaking away from the crowd glowing with festive cheer, the eager friends decided to try a little exploring on their own. Amanda and Richard quietly ventured to the staircase to make their way to the second floor. The upper floor was a void of darkness and was roped off to the public, but neither that nor the fright that suddenly took hold of

Amanda deterred them. They slowly, cautiously climbed the stairs.

Reaching the second floor landing, they suddenly drew back in surprise as their hearts skipped a beat. Standing before them in the gloom was a woman dressed in a white Victorian wedding gown! A costumed staff member? A ghost? As soon as their pulses slowed and they came to their senses, they realized it was neither, just a mannequin demonstrating 19th-century attire. Richard and Amanda exchanged sheepish grins, embarrassed by their childish fright. They took a moment to compose themselves before deciding to continue onward.

At this point, however, Amanda began to get an over-whelming feeling that their presence was not welcomed there. It felt to her as if they were intruding on someone's privacy. Amanda hugged herself tightly and shivered in the cold air. Just as she was about to turn around to leave, both friends heard the creaking of a door opening some-where in the darkened recesses of the second floor. They looked at each other in bewilderment, and they could see the fright in each other's eyes. They were sure they were alone upstairs, and their imaginations began to run wild, creating all sorts of fantastic scenarios for the noise before curiosity took hold. They wanted to see where the sound had come from. Tentatively, they walked down the hallway, deeper into the darkness. They looked on in disbelief. Not a single room on the entire second floor had a door. Impossible! If there were no doors, what had made the noise? It was definitely that of a door creaking on its hinges; both Amanda and Richard were sure of it.

At that instant a strong feeling came over Amanda, more urgent than before, telling her to leave. She instinctively sensed that they weren't wanted there. At that point, her eyes settled on what must have at one time been the master bedroom. It was a large chamber, though much of it was consumed by darkness and its details were barely discernible. Her body almost jumped out of its skin as she saw what looked like a shadow float past the window. The pale look on Richard's face told her that he had seen it as well. But it was impossible for there to have been a shadow on the window, since they were the only two people upstairs.

Amanda then saw a woman sitting at the foot of the draped bed. She hadn't been there when the friends had entered and just seemed to materialize out of the gloom. Amanda couldn't believe her eyes, and her breath felt unfamiliar and heavy in her chest. The woman was a ghost, and clearly one from many, many years ago. She seemed sad and unthreatening, but Amanda couldn't help but notice that she wore a macabre, black mourning dress. She wondered who the ghost was, who she was grieving, and why she was in this house. But Amanda also knew the spirit wasn't about to share its secrets with the living, and she whispered to Richard that it was time to go.

Finally the young friends granted the spirit her privacy. Quietly and quickly, they snuck back downstairs without letting anyone know that they had been on the second floor that had been closed to all visitors that night. On their way down, Amanda shared her vision with Richard in a voice that was as thin as the watery moonlight. Once outside and enveloped by falling snow, they stood and stared back at the house in amazement. There were so many questions, but who would answer them? One thing the two knew for certain was that they had definitely intruded on someone's private moment.

Only later did Amanda begin to wonder if perhaps the sad spirit had actually wanted someone to know the pain and sorrow that she was feeling that night. Could it have been the spirit of someone who had lived, loved and lost within that historic home? It's a question that anyone who encounters this tragic woman asks, as if knowing the details of her story will somehow make their paranormal experience easier to live with. For answers, we turn to the life of the man for whom the home is named, Doctor Charles Noble.

Charles Thompson Noble was born in 1831 on a farm in Markham Township to parents who had come to Canada from the United States some years earlier. Noble had a privileged childhood, received a fine education and graduated with a medical degree from King's College at the University of Toronto.

For a few years after graduation, Noble gained valuable practical experience as an understudy to his father, who was himself a physician. By 1856, however, he deemed himself ready to strike out on his own and headed north for Sutton.

When he arrived there, Sutton was but a small village. "It wasn't a very large place," Dr. Noble would later remember. "The whole town consisted of three hotels, a general store, a few houses and had a population of 180 persons." It was a growing community, however, and one with potential. More importantly, Sutton was a community in need of a doctor.

Not all members of the Noble family rest peacefully.

Dr. Noble was extremely well received in the town. So much so, in fact, that the community's founding family, the Bourchiers, let the young, single physician use one of their homes as a residence and medical practice. Only later would he purchase the home that today bears his family name.

A few years after arriving, Noble had the good fortune to meet Margaret Lee Johnson. He was instantly struck by the beauty and charm of the 23-year-old and began courting her enthusiastically. Soon, she too fell in love and the young couple was wed. They settled into married life easily. Dr. Noble adored his wife, and Margaret Lee proved utterly devoted to her husband and the family they created. Their first child, a daughter named Annie Lee, was born on September 26, 1864. Three years later, on September 7, 1867, a son named Charles was born.

By 1871, Dr. Noble seemingly had it all. His family life was contented, the medical practice was flourishing and he had grown quite wealthy, and the community had voted him onto the town council. Tragedy was lurking on the horizon, however, ready to strike at the idyllic family.

In 1872, Margaret learned that she was pregnant again. Both she and her husband were ecstatic at the news, and as her figure began to change their joy turned to unbridled excitement. Dr. Noble couldn't wait to see the smile on Margaret's face when she held their child for the first time; he had seen that magical moment twice before, and both times he had thought he had looked upon the face of an angel. Tragically, he wasn't to have a third heaven-sent experience.

When the baby came in April 1873, there were complications. The child, a girl, survived but Margaret began to slip away despite Dr. Noble's best efforts to keep her with him. He was frantic to save her, using all of his considerable knowledge and skill. It wasn't enough, though. Margaret Lee, the love of Dr. Noble's life, died on April 10. To honour his beloved wife, the grieving husband named the new baby Margaret. Some say he lavished extra attention on her as a result. What's certain is that he never forgot Margaret Lee and continued to cherish her memory even after he remarried years later. Their children, robbed of a mother, similarly kept her close to their hearts.

Margaret Lee Noble seems the logical identity for the distraught ghost within Noble House. Certainly there's nothing in the building's subsequent history that better fits the circumstances, lore and eyewitness accounts. Charles Thompson Noble continued to live and work out of his home until his death in 1932, just shy of his 102nd birthday and a practicing doctor to the very end. His son, a physician as well, continued to live and work out of the home, and in turn was followed by his own son. As such, Noble House remained a vibrant part of the community until very recently, when it was moved to Georgina Pioneer Village and restored to its original allure.

When this historical information was put before Amanda, her face seemed to flash with recognition. *That's it*, she thought. She had assumed that the apparition she encountered in Noble House was a woman mourning a child who had been suddenly snatched from her arms, but in fact she was grieving her own premature passing. The loss that continued to pain her all these years later was that of not being able to share memorable moments with her family, of not being able to nurture her children as they grew.

The sounds of children giggling with joy, the festive tunes floating up the stairs from the parlour below, and the holiday spirit that seemed to float upon the winter breeze—the very things Amanda and Richard found so magical about their evening at Georgina Pioneer Village—were torture to this lost soul. Imagine a Christmas spent alone, without loved ones and cherished family traditions. It would be sad and lonely, almost unbearably so. Now imagine a century of holiday seasons spent alone. That's the suffering Margaret Lee Noble endures, so it's little wonder that she wasn't a hospitable host on the evening that Amanda and Richard came calling.

Many tourists have spotted the gloomy silhouette of Margaret Lee Noble over the years. She wanders the upper floor of the building she shared with her husband and children, her long dress billowing around her ankles, a tearful look etched on her face, forever waiting to be reunited with her loved ones.

Ghosts of the Millcroft Inn and Spa

It was a cool, early winter's day when we decided to visit and research the mysteries surrounding the historic Millcroft Inn, located in the village of Alton just a few minutes outside of Orangeville. We often hear of hauntings associated with different places; even though there is a rough balance between the number of history and paranormal books we've authored, we've become known as ghost hunters, and it seems everywhere we turn someone is offering a new paranormal lead for us to follow up on. To really get in touch with a ghost story, we always feel the need to investigate the location first-hand. That's the only way we can write about it with any authority and intimacy. Unfortunately, this means that many times these reports have to be filed away for future reference. There are, after all, only so many days in a week.

It was late November 2010 when we finally got around to devoting some time to the Millcroft Inn and Spa, a property with enough paranormal activity to fill a small notebook. We drove through the snow-draped hills of Caledon and, upon arriving, were struck by the festive flourishes that abounded within the inn. Halls were decked with greenery, ornaments sparkled on their Christmas tree branches, and big bows finished off bushy wreaths. The tragedy of ghosts was temporarily forgotten.

We were shown to our rooms where we made ourselves comfortable, and after unpacking and regrouping, we headed down to meet with property manager Deborah McPherson to learn a bit of history about the inn itself. This is something that's very important to us. Knowing the history allows us to give the ghost stories we write context, providing them a solid foundation that creates a sense of authenticity and allows us to connect the past with the present in a very real way.

Deborah went beyond history to also share a number of ghost stories, both personal and from her staff members. Our notebook full, we then headed off to tour the complex. Looking around the beautifully restored buildings, feeling the warmth that embraces you as soon as you walk through the Main Mill's doors, we both agreed it was hard to believe that the Millcroft Inn is haunted. It certainly doesn't look like the prototypical haunted location our imagination conjures up. And yet, there's an unmistakable spirit to the buildings. "You can feel the energy in the buildings, as if the past continues to play out here," agreed Deborah. "At night it's even more apparent, especially in the mill."

After the informative tour, we headed to our rooms to refresh for dinner. An hour later saw us seated at a table overlooking the frozen millpond and ice-draped waterfall. It was a beautiful scene, something out of a postcard, yet Maria's face suddenly went ashen. She saw a very unhappy woman standing at the foot of the waterfall, directly below where we were seated. I looked out, my eyes straining, but I couldn't see anything in the gathering darkness of the evening. Maria began to describe the vision in stunning detail: the spirit had dark hair pulled back in a bun, and despite the frosty temperature was wearing only a white evening gown, which made Maria shiver in sympathy.

This idyllic winter wonderland was tainted by a mournful female spirit.

Of course, the young woman could not feel the cold. Alone in the night, she longs to have what was taken from her, a loved one snatched from her arms. The spirit's pain and torment were so real that Maria was almost overwhelmed. She so wanted to go and comfort her, but she knew it would be a vain effort because had she walked out there, the spectral woman would have vanished before her eyes like frosty breath.

That wasn't the end of Maria's paranormal experiences at the Millcroft Inn. Later that night, in the comfort of her room as she was getting ready for bed, she had the strangest feeling come over her. It felt as if she was being watched intently by a pair of unseen eyes. Exhausted from a long day,

Maria tried to put her discomfort aside and crawled into bed. She was just nodding off when she heard a loud knocking at her door. Thinking it was me, she reluctantly left the warmth of her bed and went to look. She unlatched the door and pulled it open, but I had not left my room, and Maria saw no sign of anyone else in the hall. It was late at night, and the building was deathly quiet and still. She closed the door and once again tried to fall asleep. Again she heard the noise at the door, taunting her. It was only with great effort that she managed to fall asleep.

Later that night, she awoke to the unmistakable sensation of someone lying beside her in the bed. While Maria was shocked, she wasn't actually scared. It felt familiar somehow; in her half-awake state, it reminded her of all those nights years ago when her young daughter, Amanda, would silently slip into her bed in the middle of the night. Maria fell back into sleep easily this time.

Now, it would be easy enough to put forward the suggestion that Maria's experiences were coloured by our meeting with Deborah McPherson or even by stories we had gathered prior to our visit, except for one inescapable fact: at that time we had heard nothing related to female ghosts anywhere on the Millcroft premises. We had heard about a wide range of inexplicable phenomena, and legends spoke of a mill-hand who fell to his death and clouded the property with his presence, but that was as much as we yet knew. It was to our surprise that we discovered numerous people had had experiences similar to Maria's, and that evidence pointed at the existence of two female spirits—one a child, one an adult woman—at the resort.

This was just one of many surprises the Millcroft Inn and Spa holds within its aged rock walls, cleverly hidden behind a joyful façade of warm hospitality, fine dining and casual luxury.

History

Strolling down the lane leading to the Millcroft Inn and Spa, an Alton resort that today exemplifies classic country charm, it's hard to imagine that this pretty site was once a bustling industrial hub. However, from the 1880s to the 1960s, it was one of the leading knitting mills in all of Canada, manufacturing all manner of woollen garments that were shipped across the country and overseas.

Huddled along the banks of Shaw's Creek, the resort consists of a collection of century-old buildings that have retained much of their original appearance and charm. It's apparent from the moment you arrive that this place is rich in history, and soon you find yourself wondering, if walls could talk, what fascinating tales the Millcroft Inn would tell.

Milling began on site as early as 1845, when William McClellan built a wood frame building to produce yarn and blankets. Sometime around 1875, Benjamin Ward moved to Alton when his woollen mill in Cataract burned to the ground. He bought the McClellan operation and replaced the existing mill with a far more substantial, four storey structure built of beautiful stone quarried in nearby

Inglewood. Ward's son-in-law, John M. Dods, purchased the mill in 1892. Dods was an enterprising, ambitious, well-educated and mechanically inclined individual—the type of man who drove progress through willpower and vision. After he assumed control of the operation, he transformed it into one of the largest producers of wool garments in the country.

The mill could barely keep up with demand, and any setback in production chafed at Dods. Even the slightest delay frustrated the driven businessman, so one can imagine the bouts of anger and dismay he suffered through every time a flood or a fire—both of which plagued early mills with regularity—threatened his business. At least three times during the period 1880–1900, Shaw's Creek flooded and caused extensive damage to the mill.

Fire, though less frequent, was even more devastating to early mills. The Dods Knitting Mill (as the enterprise had become known) was particularly at risk because of its coal-fired steam generator: more efficient than relying on waterpower, but far more unstable. Dods dodged fate for almost three decades, but it eventually caught up with him in 1917, when a disastrous fire gutted his mill. The fire couldn't have come at a worse time. Canada was fighting the First World War, and Dods had received huge contracts to supply the army with socks, underwear, blankets and other assorted woollen gear. Neither he nor the army he was supplying could afford a let-down in productivity.

As a result, as soon as the smoke had cleared after the fire, Dods rebuilt. Precautions were made to avoid a repeat. The third floor of the mill became a water tower and an expensive sprinkler system was added. When John Dods died in 1923, the mill was back up to full capacity and was once again one of the leading woollen goods manufacturers in Canada.

The Dods Knitting Mill continued to operate under the stewardship of Dods' sons, James and Andrew. In fact, it experienced a new renaissance during World War II (1939–1945), when it once again was asked to outfit hundreds of thousands of men and women in the armed forces. During this period, and for the first time ever, the majority of the employees at the mill were women.

Unfortunately, that was the peak of the mill's fortunes. The post-war years were less kind. Increased overseas competition and the increasingly widespread use of synthetic materials slowly ate away at its profits and eroded its markets. With each passing year it became more and more obvious that the mill, at some undetermined point in the future, would have to cave to the inevitable and close. That day came in 1965. The mill closed for good. It was the end of an era, and a sad day for employees and residents of the community alike. The mill had been a landmark in Alton. At that time, they couldn't have foreseen that 40 years later the mill would still be a landmark, though now in the guise of a charming country inn.

The Millcroft today is a four-diamond resort that brilliantly blends rustic charm true to its heritage with the dramatic opulence of a world-class resort and spectacular natural scenery. Today, the Main Mill houses the inn's main lobby, a fine-dining restaurant and 22 guest rooms, 10 of which have views of the falls and river below. While the mill's interior has been extensively renovated over the years to accommodate modern luxuries, its exterior has changed little in the past century. Across the laneway is a handsome stone conference centre, formerly a warehouse. Just beyond, surrounded by immaculate formal gardens, is the manor home where the Dods family lived, now home to a number of luxurious guest accommodations.

The Millcroft Inn is most certainly not the sort of place that one would instantly associate with ghosts, yet there are dozens of reports, dating back decades, wherein a staff member or guest unexpectedly had a supernatural encounter. The registry lists at least four spectral guests who refuse to check out: a shadowy entity that may be reliving a painful death and seeking assistance from the living; a phantom child in search of playmates; the long departed mill owner, who just can't let go of the business he built; and the apparition of a beautiful but mournful woman who wanders the mill, perhaps looking for a lost loved one.

"Alton is so old and has so much history that there's bound to be ghosts here," says Deborah McPherson, the inn's property manager. "At one time, Alton was bigger and more important than Orangeville. It was a bustling town and a lot happened here. Maybe that's why so many buildings in town are haunted. The Alton Mill is said to have a ghost, and we certainly have our own. It's a spiritually active village."

That connection to history and spirits from the past makes any stay at the Millcroft Inn a truly memorable experience.

The Main Mill

The Main Mill at the Millcroft Inn, the heart of the resort's operation, has seen its share of haunting phenomena over the years, as told by employees—both past and present—and many guests. Some of the stories are truly chilling. And yet, when you enter the building you feel warmed by nostalgia and hospitality. It's an almost surreal contrast that makes the Millcroft Inn all the more fascinating.

Stories of strange sounds in the middle of the night and ghostly apparitions floating upon breezes go back as far as anyone can remember, but it's possible the renovation that saw the abandoned and silent mill turned into a restaurant in the 1970s was responsible for disturbing restful spirits, causing them to rise up along with the unsettled dust. Certainly, we know that the ghosts become more active and the experiences reported by eyewitnesses more intense whenever there is a fresh round of renovations.

Charles Banfield, a former marketing manager at the Millcroft Inn, recounts one memorable episode. "There was a puzzling incident that occurred a few years back when the Millcroft Dam, over which the water flows in a gorgeous spectacle, was being refurbished. A cement machine that was being used to pour in the new concrete suddenly stopped working shortly after work started. The mechanics who came to the site couldn't figure out what the problem was, so the rest of the cement to finish the dam had to be ported and poured via wheelbarrow. When the equipment was removed from the Millcroft property it suddenly started to working again." No one could ever come up with an explanation that satisfied those who had witnessed the event.

The list of paranormal activity that has taken place in and around the mill is lengthy. It includes a guest who took photos of unnatural wisps of smoke rising like spectral tentacles from the ground just outside, the sudden appearance and equally sudden disappearance of a spectral Indian wandering around the pond or standing in the archway of the ruined dye building across the stream, unusual sounds echoing through the building at all hours of the night, and poltergeist activity in guest rooms.

The Main Mill is home to two female ghosts.

A function room occupies the lowest level of the building, where in years past there would have been a web of pulleys and belts. In later years, these were kept going by a coal-powered boiler, but originally the woollen mill's machinery was powered by a single water-driven turbine, parts of which remain and can be seen from the balcony off of the room. All of this equipment has long since been removed to make way for a space where weddings and other parties can be held. And yet, the echoes remain: the clanking and grinding of gears and pulleys coming from the basement, and the sloshing of water over a wheel that has long since been removed, are still occasionally heard to this day.

A waitress informed us that a group of serious "suit-and-tie-type" businessmen visiting the inn for a convention all distinctly heard the sounds of milling machinery echoing up from the room below. They were eager to see the machinery in operation and excitedly asked her if they were able to go downstairs and watch. Slightly confused, she patiently told the men that there was no machinery to be seen. They refused to believe that the gears, pulleys and other machines they all adamantly insisted they heard hadn't been present for four decades. In fact, it was only after the waitress guided them down the stairs, showing them the function room where the machinery used to be located, that the men reluctantly accepted her word.

Jill Sproule, a former property manager, had numerous unusual experiences while working at the inn. She has no doubt that the building is haunted. "This building has an energy that you can feel, probably tied to its history. There are a lot of strange noises in the building at night. This building talks at night, almost as if it is whispering a secret or letting us know spirits are amongst us," she said over a cup of coffee. "There may be several spirits. One I know of is a young woman with high, laced-up boots who is often seen in the dining room. The night audit people see her a lot. Some staff members have seen a female figure in the upstairs rooms as well. I think I may have seen her once, out of the corner of my eye. She looked more like a child than a woman, but I suppose she may have been a teenaged girl."

Indeed, there seem to be two distinct female ghosts who enjoy the comfortable confines of the Main Mill building. One is a beautiful woman, an adult but not quite middle-aged, so likely between 20 and 40 years old. Despite her beauty, her most distinctive characteristic is the sadness that clouds her features. Many people who witness her feel an overwhelming sense of loss and are brought to the verge of tears. Some have postulated that this woman may be the first wife of John Dods, who died in childbirth.

The other apparition is much younger, perhaps even still a child, and may be the same girl seen so often in the Manor House (see page 207 for more). It seems she may wander from building to building as her youthful whims dictate. Why not? In life children are notoriously difficult to place restrictions on, so why would it be any different in death? This undead girl is no more likely to remain bound to a single building than a child might willingly accept being banished to her room in punishment.

One experience with this young girl was particularly powerful. When we spoke to a former guest named Deb (not to be confused with Deborah McPherson), it was clear the emotion of that evening—fear, sadness, shock—was still very strong even though a few months had passed.

The events she related took place in January 2009. It was a night marked by particularly foul winter weather. Wind howled through the trees, scrabbling at the walls of the inn. Shards of ice clattered against the window as sleet and snow fell steadily, a frigid downpour that clung to the roof and trees in ever-thickening sheets.

Around 11 PM, Deb slowly slipped her tired body into the warm and comforting bed that she had been so looking forward to the whole day. Despite the serenity and beauty of the historical inn, the young woman was exhausted from a full-day conference. She and her coworker had agreed to meet up for breakfast early in the morning, so sleep was the only thing on her mind as she closed her eyes. "I crawled into bed and had started to fall asleep when the room began to grow abnormally cold. The thermostat was up high and the heater was on, and yet I was freezing. I would describe it as a supernatural chill," she recalled.

The cold caused Deb to bury herself in blankets, shivering uncontrollably. If her arm slipped out from under the comforter it would be covered in goose bumps instantly, sending a gnawing cold through her body. The cold was almost unbearable. As hard as she tried to summon sleep, she couldn't get warm enough to feel comfortable enough to nod off. It felt like a cloak of cold air was wrapped around her instead of the warm blankets that she actually lay under.

"Suddenly, and to my horror, I felt the weight of someone sitting on the edge of my bed. I was shivering with cold and fright, and I didn't dare bring my head out from under the blankets," Deb continued. "Slowly, the weight shifted, and it began to move up the other side of the bed. It was getting closer, closer. I could swear the weight laid down beside me, curled on the bed as if to sleep. I didn't move, but my fear and the cold began to subside, transforming into compassion and then even love as I felt the small form of a child lying beside me. I somehow knew the ghost sharing my bed was a young, innocent girl who was scared and needed companionship. She was alone and was terribly sad."

Deb wanted to reach out and comfort the child, to wrap her in her arms and protect her from whatever she was afraid of. But as she reached out an arm to do so, the young child disappeared. As fast as she had first appeared, she was gone. Deb fell asleep soon after that, but it wasn't so easy to shake off the effects of the ghostly encounter. The sense of sadness and loss darkened her mood for several days, and even two months later, talking about it was hard. Deb believes the spirit died young and, as a result of a life unfulfilled, is restless.

While ghostly experiences such as Deb's are hardly common occurrences at the Millcroft Inn, the mere possibility that a guest *might* have a paranormal encounter only adds to the inn's historical ambience and considerable charm. If a spirit does choose to share your accommodations, be respectful. After all, guests come and go, but for the ghosts, the inn is home.

The Manor House

The Manor House is a charming building with heritage-inspired accommodations, but it is equally well known for its unexplained phenomena. Perhaps this is only natural, seeing as how it was once the private home of John Dods and his family. His wealth and standing are reflected in the grandeur of the building, which undoubtedly was the largest and finest house in Alton. If indeed the industrialist or a member of his family is tied to the property, it only makes sense that they should make themselves comfortable in their former home. And who could blame them? The home is magnificent, the rooms are charming, and the heritage gardens out front are a peaceful oasis.

A spectral girl causes mischief in the Manor House.

If the stories told over the years are true (and many of them came from highly reputable individuals), at least one member of the family does remain in residence to this day, sharing the luxurious accommodations with mortal guests.

Strange and inexplicable sounds are heard, and items move as if manipulated by unseen hands. A room suddenly and mysteriously becomes chokingly foul-smelling. A television turns on and off by itself throughout the night. Most people think the spirit responsible is a young girl who playfully haunts the building. She runs down the halls at all hours of the night, plays mischievous tricks on unsuspecting guests, and on one occasion startled a guest by saying hello in her ear while remaining invisible.

Alton legend has a tale to explain the haunting. The story goes that a young girl fell from a second floor window while playing and landed horribly on the ground below, her little bones no match for the fall. Her parents heard her desperate cries and raced to her side, cradling her broken body as she slipped away, a life tragically cut far too short. One can only imagine the wounds that would have cut deep into her parents' hearts upon watching their beloved daughter die in their arms.

This is certainly a heart-wrenching story, but is it true? Benjamin Ward built the home around 1875 and resided there with his family for a number of years. Records for his family are spotty, but there is no sign of a girl dying either within its brick walls or otherwise. In 1892, John Dods, his wife Fanny Ward (Benjamin's daughter) and their three children moved into the house. Shortly afterward the couple's fourth child, a daughter named Dorothy, was born. Tragically, Fanny died bringing her into the world. For years, the sound of Dorothy's little feet racing through the home was a familiar one. She was joined in her playful antics by two more siblings, James and Margaret, after her father married Cora Barber.

So while there is as yet no evidence of a child dying on site, it's possible the spectral girl in a frilly dress and sun hat is one of the Dods children, perhaps one who refuses to let go of an attachment to the beloved family home in which she experienced her most joyful memories. Of the four Dods girls, only Dorothy and Margaret were born in the Alton home, and it seems possible one of them has never left, retaining her ties to it in death and reverting back to a happy childhood.

Some people suggest that there is a darker, sadder explanation. The night that Dorothy entered the world was a traumatic one. We imagine that Fanny was wracked by pain as she lay in bed, feverish, drenched with sweat. With failing strength, she propped herself up on her pillows yet again and urged her child to come, crying with the exertion. Her pains fell short of their purpose. She fell back onto the bed, pale as a wraith. A shadow of despair crossed her face. Fanny knew either she or her child would not survive the ordeal, and prayed to God that he would take her in the baby's stead. Her silent prayers were granted.

Fanny died of her strenuous labour, leaving Dorothy to grow up without the loving care of her natural mother. She never knew what it was like to be cradled in a mother's arms, or to fall asleep to a gentle voice singing a lullaby. Her father later remarried, but no stepmother—no matter how kind and warm—could take the place of her birth mother. As a result, there was undoubtedly a void in Dorothy's life. It's possible that the psychic scars of growing up without a mother, and even in a way being responsible for her mother's death, have imprisoned Dorothy's soul within the building and caused her to revert to childhood, a time when she often longed for her mother. Perhaps she is trying to reconnect with her mother's spirit; some believe the ghostly lady haunting the property is indeed Fanny Dods (refer back to The Main Mill, page 201).

Whoever the Manor House's spectral girl may be, Deborah McPherson, the Millcroft Inn's property manager, believes she might have had an encounter with her. "The Manor House has a young girl ghost, five to six years old, in a white ruffled dress, white stockings, shiny black shoes and white wide-brimmed hat. She is most often seen—in a fleeting moment—going into a room on the second floor. I saw her once so I know the stories are true. It was only for a few seconds but she was definitely there." Although this is merely speculation, the girl's clothing seems to be of the Victorian era, which would seem to lend some credibility to the theory that she is related to John Dods.

The occasional appearance of a cute-as-a-button little girl wouldn't alarm most people, even if the girl did fade through walls or vanish into thin air. But there's more. "This is the heart of most haunts at the mill," explains a former employee at the inn. "I had heard about and saw a stack of complaint cards behind the front desk regarding the Manor House, from seeing apparitions and hearing unusual sounds to experiencing cold drafts and even odd smells." On one complaint card, a guest wrote about a lamp in his room that rocked back and forth on its own. There was no draft, no vibration in the building that might cause the lamp to move in that manner. It was a mystery, and strangely enough the man discovered the lamp only moved when the room was in darkness; as soon as the room was illuminated, the lamp stopped its inexplicable rocking.

Sometimes the paranormal activities occurred when least expected, explained the former employee. Late one evening, long after all the guests had gone to their rooms and the inn was locked up, the man accompanied the night auditor to the Manor House's penthouse suite, which, he was told, was often the scene of strange phenomena. "I almost immediately felt uncomfortable [in the suite]. No cold drafts or anything of this nature, but simply felt as if one or more additional people were in the room with us," he relates. "After about five minutes, a garbage can underneath a counter started making tapping sounds, not too loud, but it sounded as if someone was knocking on it with fingers. I got up enough nerve to pick it up—and it continued tapping in my hands. I could feel very light knocks to the metal, which made me extremely uncomfortable. It was a very uneasy experience, as I never thought I'd experience something like this first-hand. The can stopped tapping a few minutes after I put it back down."

Guests are as likely as staff members to encounter the ghostly child. It doesn't matter who you are—a young couple simply trying to get away from the stress of everyday life, a businessman planning his next business deal, male or female—the lost girl is equally likely to pay anyone a visit. With the innocence of youth, she plays no favourites.

In 2006, a newlywed couple, "Trish" and "John," elected to escape the city by heading north into the tranquil Caledon Hills and booking a three-day weekend at the Millcroft Inn. They chose a room in the Manor House, lured by its history, tastefully appointed rooms, antique furnishings and serene views overlooking landscaped Victorian gardens. After settling into their room, and being tempted by the jetted tub in their bathroom, the couple changed into casual clothes and headed out to explore some of the trails that weave through the wooded property. When Trish and John returned, tired but exhila-rated, they stopped before the door to their room; they could hear walking and shuffling sounds on the other side. At first they were alarmed, but then they decided it was probably housekeeping letting down the bed. Opening the door, they were shocked to find no one there. The room was empty.

Later that evening, having returned from an enjoyable dinner overlooking the rushing waterfall of Shaw's Creek, they returned to once again hear the same walking and shuf-fling within their room. As before, as soon as they entered the sounds stopped. It happened one final time, late at night while the couple was in bed sleeping. Trish woke to the now familiar sounds, this time only a few feet away.

For a moment she dared not move, clinging to the blankets as if it were a matter of life and death. She was terrified. When at last the paralysis wore off and she shook John awake, the sounds mysteriously ceased. That was the last time the invisible visitor wandered through their room; the next two days passed uneventfully, and by the time they left it was the intimate ambience rather than the ghostly phenomenon of the first day that stood out.

More recently, Emily, a hostess in the inn's dining room, had a man share his own encounter with the spirit, and she in turn shared it with us: "We had a lawyer here who asked me one day if we had a ghost in the Manor House. When I said yes and asked why, he claimed to have sensed a presence in his room all night long. He didn't see anything, but he felt someone there with him. He's a lawyer, a professional, not the type to make something like that up, so I definitely believed him," she said. Her story just proves that anyone who comes to the Millcroft Inn with an open mind may get a sense of the various ghosts in residence.

Numerous such stories, unusual but hardly horrifying, have surfaced over the years. Within this elegant old house, the door to the afterlife occasionally creaks open and a long-dead little girl—perhaps one who suffered an agonizing and untimely death—steps through into our world. She proves the emotional link between a person and her home can be strong enough to reach beyond the grave.

John M. Dods and his Undead Employee

It seems that all of the buildings that today comprise the Millcroft Inn and Spa have a paranormal story or two to tell. The Millcroft Conference Centre is a popular place for business leaders and their employees to hold their meetings away from the familiar stresses of the workplace. Mixing business with pleasure is easily achieved here as businesses attempt to boost team spirit. But these meetings occasionally end up with an uninvited guest or two, and visitors to the conference centre are often greeted by a dark figure who stares mournfully out from a window on the building's second floor.

The conference centre was formerly the mill's warehouse, where woollen garments were stored before being shipped to distant markets. At one point an elevated steel catwalk ran from the mill to the warehouse, designed to make it easier to transfer finished goods between the two buildings. Along with the main mill, this building was ravaged by fire in 1917, and if you know where to look, flame-blackened bricks can still be seen within.

Today, instead of housing woollen undergarments ready to be shipped, the one-time warehouse is home to a wide range of inexplicable activity. At night, while all is silent and guests are comfortably sleeping in their rooms, staff members of the Millcroft Inn have reportedly heard heavy footsteps from the second floor of the conference centre, like those of a man with a heavy step and determination to oversee the comings and goings of the place.

And in addition to the figure looming at the window and the sounds of the footsteps, at least one conference guest saw unnatural shadows eerily creeping across the walls of the building.

It is believed that these phenomena are perpetrated by not one, but rather two distinct ghosts. One is suspected to be former owner John Dods, who died suddenly and unexpectedly in 1923 while conducting business in Montreal. He was only 57 years old. His death shook the community to the core. But perhaps Dods isn't truly gone. Is he the figure who looks out onto the property, unwilling to completely abandon the business he so painstakingly built? Most people describe the ghost as being a handsome and distinguished gentleman, which would certainly seem to point the finger at Dods.

The second spirit is a melancholy ghost, likely that of a former employee who met a tragic death while working at the mill. He was crossing the bridge from the mill to the warehouse when he lost his balance and fell over the railing. He dropped more than 40 feet to the ground below, breaking limbs and driving shattered ribs like spears into his body. Warm blood began to flow from his body, pooling in a crimson puddle around him. The pain was so intense that he drifted into unconsciousness and, after lingering in terrible agony for a few hours, finally slipped into eternal sleep. But though the man may have died, there are some who believe his spirit remained, clinging to the warehouse's walls like spectral moss. It wasn't long after his death that rumours of ghostly goings-on began to surface, and over the years they have only multiplied. Has he joined Dods at the Millcroft Inn, returning to the job that cost him his life?

An unidentified member of Torontoghosts, a team of supernatural investigators, was formerly an employee of the Millcroft Inn. He wrote about his experiences on the organization's website and shed some light on the shadowy goings-on within the one-time warehouse. He generally worked the overnight shift, when nothing exciting ever seemed to happen. On one of his late nights, this man was asked by another employee if he would like to see the paranormal hot-spots of the inn. In an effort to alleviate his creeping boredom, he enthusiastically agreed. The man was excited by the possibility of experiencing a ghost encounter for himself since he had heard so much about the inn's history and its mysterious activities.

"He [the other employee] took me outside and crossed to the conference centre. We walked through the front doors, when he stopped and said, 'Just wait,'" the Torontoghosts member writes. "We stopped in silence waiting for something to happen. Sure enough, about a minute later we heard faint, then heavy footsteps from amongst the ducts running throughout the conference centre. However, they seemed to be initiated from the second floor. This is a regular occurrence that he heard nearly every night while making his rounds. There is no mistake as to the sounds…they are definitely footsteps."

In addition to hearing disembodied footsteps, the other employee also claimed to have seen a figure standing in the window, often when making the rounds of the property at night. The dark figure would simply stare out the window in frozen interest, looking straight ahead, as still as a statue. In the faint glow of the streetlight, the employee could determine that the looming figure was a man dressed in formal but old-fashioned clothes. Eventually, the spirit would fade into nothingness. "Unfortunately, I never saw this myself," writes the Torontoghosts member, clearly regretting a missed opportunity.

Dusk fell early on the October day in 2009 when a pair of guests had a haunting experience outside the conference centre. Dark shadows were like inky pools beneath the trees that lined the drive, and clouds blotted out the stars and moon above. Jen and her husband stepped quickly from the Main Mill, where they had just finished a pleasant dinner, and walked briskly across the road to the pathway leading to their room in the Manor House. They were midway across when Jen stopped abruptly, startled. She pointed a quivering finger to a spot just ahead. What seemed like a large, vaguely man-shaped shadow on the ground suddenly slithered into action, snaking across the drive and in under the door to the conference centre. It was brief but unmistakable, and terribly frightening for them both.

The activities of these two ghosts aren't confined to the conference centre. As previously mentioned, long ago there was a steel catwalk that connected the mill and what was then the warehouse. You could walk from one building to the other with ease, and so the entities continue the same routine today. Several sightings have taken place in the Main Mill's guest rooms, most of them on the third floor where the catwalk would have emerged.

Maura, who stayed in a guest room on the third floor of the inn, had an experience she would not soon forget. The event took place in March 2007, but it was so horrifying that it was still fresh in her mind when we interviewed her more than four years later. "I felt really cold. That was the first thing I noticed when I woke up in the middle of the night. Then the door opened with a spine-chilling creak. I was sure I locked it before going to bed, but I heard it open and saw a sliver of a dim light enter the room. 'No, no,' I thought. 'This can't be happening.' I closed my eyes, hoping I was just dreaming."

Maura squeezed her eyes closed and willed herself to wake from what was building up to be a nightmare. When she finally had the courage to open her eyes, she noticed that she obviously hadn't wakened. The stream of light was still coming in through the door that was still open. She then became aware of a dark, shadowy figure standing in the corner of the room. She couldn't make out his features, except for the fact that he was a frail-looking man with dark hair matted to his head and a straggly beard. He looked at Maura, accusingly almost, in the manner that one would look at someone who has invaded their home. The apparition just stood there motionless and watched with eyes hidden by shadow as she lay in her bed, shaking with fear. Terrified into paralysis, she couldn't even call out for help. Hard as she tried, nothing, not a sound, came out.

The ominous figure continued to linger, looking intently at the shivering woman. Maura suddenly noticed that the spectral intruder was physically disfigured and didn't seem to be standing straight. It was as though he had suffered some sort of accident that left his body broken and misshapen. Maybe the spirit heard Maura's thoughts because he suddenly cried out in a whispery voice, "Help me, please." Maura jumped from the bed and to her feet, stifling a scream of terror. In that instant, the ghost floated to the doorway and a skeletal hand commanded the creaking door to close behind him. It protested sharply, reluctant to shut the portal between our realm and that of the dead. "I just stood there, frozen to my spot, and could not believe what had just happened. All I knew was that I wouldn't sleep the rest of the night. How could I? It was terrifying," she recalls.

Could this late-night visitor have been the long-lost employee who fell to his death? Was he attempting to call out to someone—anyone—who might hear his cries for help? That March night was certainly frightening, and yet, if you ask Maura, she wouldn't give up the experience. To know with certainty that something exists beyond death is a gift, she believes, and in retrospect she realizes the ghost meant her no harm. He was simply looking for someone to end the agony and torment that is his existence.

Ghosts are usually tied to events in the past, and with the Millcroft Inn and Spa being so rich in history, one cannot always be sure who the ghosts they see floating among the rooms might have been. What's certain is that both John Dods and the worker who fell to his death had unusually strong emotional bonds to the buildings. One viewed the mill as a proud legacy, the result of a lifetime of hard work. The other suffered an untimely demise there, dying in a horribly painful and tragic manner. Both men, therefore, had very good reason to remain spiritually bound to the Millcroft buildings, even after death had claimed their bodies.

Acknowledgements

The authors wish to acknowledge the helpful staff at Ontario's fine archives, museums and public libraries. Without their expertise, assistance and enthusiastic support, researching the historical foundations of the stories within this book would have been immeasurably more difficult and time consuming. Of particular note is Bruce Beacock of the Simcoe County Archives, who has always been generous with his time and resources. It's long past due that he be recognized.

Many other people provided assistance in the preparation of this book. Without their contributions, *More Ontario Ghost Stories* would not have been possible. Foremost among these individuals are Diane Turner, Deborah McPherson and the entirety of the staff at the Millcroft Inn and Spa, who we wish to thank both for offering their ghostly experiences and for their warm hospitality at one of the provinces's finest hotels. Other people who notably helped include Geri Smith and the staff of Black Creek Pioneer Village; Bill Brodeur of Huronia Historical Parks, who provided guided tours and a wealth of information on Discovery Harbour and Sainte-Marie among the Hurons, during which his passion for these sites rubbed off on us; Elaine Bald, formerly theatre director of Niagara's IMAX Theatre; Philip Rose Donohue and Melissa Matt at Georgina Pioneer Village and Archives; Sue St. Clair of the Toronto Ghosts and Hauntings Research Society, who was so generous with her knowledge and research, proving that those with a passion for the paranormal comprise a true community; and Wendy and Dave Barrer of Heritage Homestead.

Perhaps most importantly, we would like to thank all those people who bravely stepped forward to share with us their encounters with the supernatural. One runs the risk of ridicule by doing so, and we applaud their courage and extend a heartfelt thank you for their unique contributions to this book. Their experiences provide the stories appearing in *More Ontario Ghost Stories* with an intimacy and richness of detail that could not otherwise have been created. If while reading this book you feel a tingle in your spine, discover your pulse is racing or find your sleep interrupted by nightmares, it's thanks to them.

Finally, we would like to once again thank Nancy Foulds at Ghost House Books for allowing us to write *More Ontario Ghost Stories*. We have wanted to share with readers the stories collected within this book for a long time; thanks to her faith in us, we're now able to do so. Thank you, Nancy.

Personal Acknowledgements

Andrew Hind writes: Ontario is a vast province with a rich treasure trove of historic sites and restless souls—if you know where to look. Discovering these stories, and sharing them with readers, has been an amazing experience. They are too many to mention by name, but suffice it to say everyone who provided a tidbit of information, a lead to follow, a haunting story or even a word of encouragement helped in some small way to making this book a reality.

I also want to extend a warm thank you to Maria for exploring the dark recesses of Ontario with me. You never know what you'll find when poking into the shadows, but thanks to her, instead of lurking monsters or undead crawling forth from ancient graves, I can truthfully say I found only joy and new memories to cherish.

Maria Da Silva writes: After reading a very chilling book called *The Entity* when I was about thirteen, I became deeply fascinated with the paranormal. After having many deja-vu moments and experiencing several unexplainable incidents, I can now, in my later years, be proud to say I honestly believe in the existence of ghosts. For those of you who don't believe, you don't know what you're missing...it's a life-changing experience. Thank you to Andrew and our publishing company for allowing me to share my passion for the supernatural with readers.

About the Authors

Maria Da Silva and **Andrew Hind** are freelance writers who specialize in the paranormal, history and travel. They have a passion for bringing to light unusual stories, little-known episodes in history and fascinating locations few people know about. Together, they have contributed numerous articles to magazine publications and newspapers, including the *Toronto Star*, *Lakeland Boating*, *Horizons*, *Niagara Life*, *Muskoka Magazine* and *History Magazine*, and they write regular features for *Paranormal Magazine*. They also conduct guided historical and ghost tours, helping people connect with the past in a personal way. Their previous books include *Cottage Country Ghosts* (Ghost House Books) and *Niagara: Daredevils, Danger and Extraordinary Stories* (Folklore Press).

Maria has always had a passion for ghosts and the paranormal. Her interest in the subject and the joy she finds in travelling inspired *More Ontario Ghost Stories*. Andrew developed a love of history early on, and he hopes, through his writing, to develop a similar passion in others. *More Ontario Ghost Stories* is Maria and Andrew's tenth book.